# VICKIE HOWELL'S
# POP GOES CROCHET!

# VICKIE HOWELL'S
# POP GOES CROCHET

## 36 PROJECTS INSPIRED BY ICONS OF POPULAR CULTURE

# LARK BOOKS

A Division of Sterling Publishing Co., Inc.
New York / London

SENIOR EDITOR: **VALERIE VAN ARSDALE SHRADER**
EDITOR: **NATHALIE MORNU**
ART DIRECTOR: **KRISTI PFEFFER**
PHOTOGRAPHER: **STEWART O'SHIELDS**
COVER DESIGNER: **ERIC STEVENS**
ILLUSTRATOR: **ORRIN LUNDGREN**
ADDITIONAL BACKGROUND PHOTOGRAPHY:
**MEGAN COX, STEWART O'SHIELDS,
KRISTI PFEFFER, SHANNON YOKELEY**

For the crocheters,
knitters, and
crafters—both friends
and fans
alike—whose
unwavering support
has enriched
my life, career,
and community.
Thank you.

Library of Congress Cataloging-in-Publication Data

Howell, Vickie.
 Vickie Howell's pop goes crochet : celebrating icons of popular culture. -- 1st ed.
  p. cm.
 Includes index.
 ISBN 978-1-60059-466-3 (pb-pbk. with flaps : alk. paper)
 1. Crocheting--Patterns. 2. Celebrities. I. Title. II. Title: Pop goes crochet.
 TT825.H685 2009
 746.43'4041--dc22

                                    2008036242

10 9 8 7 6 5 4 3 2 1

First Edition

Published by Lark Books, A Division of
Sterling Publishing Co., Inc.
387 Park Avenue South, New York, NY 10016

Text © 2009, Vickie Howell
Photography © 2009, Lark Books unless otherwise specified
Illustrations © 2009, Lark Books

Distributed in Canada by Sterling Publishing,
c/o Canadian Manda Group, 165 Dufferin Street
Toronto, Ontario, Canada M6K 3H6

Distributed in the United Kingdom by GMC Distribution Services,
Castle Place, 166 High Street, Lewes, East Sussex, England BN7 1XU

Distributed in Australia by Capricorn Link (Australia) Pty Ltd.,
P.O. Box 704, Windsor, NSW 2756 Australia

If you have questions or comments about this book, please contact:
Lark Books
67 Broadway
Asheville, NC 28801
828-253-0467

Manufactured in China

ISBN 13: 978-1-60059-466-3

For information about custom editions, special sales, or premium and corporate purchases, please
contact the Sterling Special Sales Department at 800 805-5489 or specialsales@sterlingpub.com.

# Vickie Howell's
## POP GOES CROCHET!

**popular culture.** *n.* The prevailing vernacular culture in any given society, including art, cooking, clothing, entertainment, mass media, music, and style.

—Allwords.com

**crochet.** *v.intr.* To make a piece of needlework by looping thread with a hooked needle. *v.tr.* To make by looping thread with a hooked needle: crochet a sweater. *n.* Needlework made by looping thread with a hooked needle.

—thefreedictionary.com

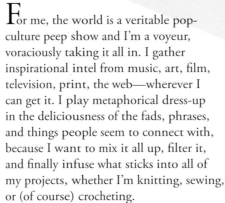

*I'm a culture vulture, and I just want to experience it all.*

—Debbie Harry

For me, the world is a veritable pop-culture peep show and I'm a voyeur, voraciously taking it all in. I gather inspirational intel from music, art, film, television, print, the web—wherever I can get it. I play metaphorical dress-up in the deliciousness of the fads, phrases, and things people seem to connect with, because I want to mix it all up, filter it, and finally infuse what sticks into all of my projects, whether I'm knitting, sewing, or (of course) crocheting.

You see, popular culture, which now includes even politics thanks to the brilliant minds of Jon Stewart and Stephen Colbert, is a *uniter*. It's a form of history not based on just particular dates and events but also on the commercials we heard, the clothes we wore, and the songs we sang during a particular moment in time—and just as important, it's history based on how these things made us *feel*.

Martha Stewart holding the infamous poncho crocheted by a fellow inmate; the crafting mogul wore it on the day of her 2005 release.

Mary Altaffer/Associated Press

Sometimes seemingly insignificant impressions make a statement about society and our own interaction with it. Here's what I mean:

* Ever get a nostalgic grin when you remember an old commercial jingle advertising a magically delicious (but probably not too healthy) cereal? We were less health-conscious back in the day, weren't we?

* Maybe you celebrated the end of the grunge era in the late '90s by proudly parading around with a new haircut inspired by a very "friendly" TV show.

* Are you anxious about hanging chads when you vote? The 2000 election, with all the turmoil surrounding it, may still be on your mind.

* Perhaps you let out a happy sigh whenever a pop star or a couple of gorgeous actors add another child to their brood; their embrace of an evolving definition of family also enhances our global awareness.

So admit it—pop culture has and will continue to touch our lives ... whether we like it or not.

*The whole celebrity culture thing—I'm fascinated by, and repelled by, and yet I end up knowing about it.*

—Anderson Cooper

How does all this relate to crochet, you might ask? If pop culture influences everything we do, that includes our craft. And historically, crochet has always reflected the times it lived in.

In the '20s, when excess reigned, small crocheted and beaded bags swung from the wrists of flappers who needed a little something to hold their lipsticks while they Charlestoned the night away. As times changed, so did the medium. World War II demanded a frugality in both living and stitching, so crocheters used their yarn sparingly in small projects like handkerchiefs and scarves.

Ode to Ms. Diaz's beachy style: the "Cameron" Hoodie

The princess of neo-soul style inspired the Erykah coat on page 130.

John Spellman/Retna Ltd.

Chris Walter/WireImage/Getty Images

Bob Marley sports his renowned Rasta tam.

*Today's crafters have taken it much further, using crochet in new, unexpected, and even subversive ways....*

In the conservative '50s, the prim and proper cardigan held center stage, but in the volatile '60s we let it all hang out; the counterculture ruled and handicrafts were where it was at. Ponchos and airy crocheted vests were seen on the likes of Janis Joplin, who frequently rocked both of these garments. Today's crafters have taken it much further, using crochet in new, unexpected, and even subversive ways—in response to global warming, crocheters have created an entire coral reef from yarn; others proudly create crocheted cozies for their birth control devices. Getting the picture?

The popularity of crochet is growing and speaks loudly to me about the state of the current social climate. Everyone from game show queen Vanna White to rock bassist Eddie Breckenridge has started stitching, because crochet offers self-expression through design and color choices and it acts as a form of stress relief. Beyond that, though, every hand-made piece has the ability to produce something positive for the world. Quite simply, crochet feeds the human need for balance in our lives. Making something with our hands reflects something basic

Psst, c'mon,
take a peek with me.

about ourselves. We want to work hard without losing touch with our creative selves; we want to earn money without losing our souls; and we want to be a part of a larger picture of human progression while still maintaining our individuality. Crochet, like all craft, lends itself as a means to that ultimate goal. (And thanks to Internet storefronts, it even brings in a little cash for those wanting to sell their crocheted wares.)

Because so many people are using crochet to make a personal statement, you'll find an abundance of images of it in print, on the tube, and onscreen. Icons from Martha to Madonna have been famously photographed wearing crochet, and countless contemporary movies feature it in wardrobes or sets; just check out *Charlie and the Chocolate Factory*, *Sweeney Todd* (oh, Tim Burton, how I *heart* you!), *Notes on a Scandal*, and *Spider-Man*, to name a few. My friends, this means that crochet has seeped into our collective cultural psyche!

Join me by taking a peek at pop culture through stitchers' eyes as we pay tribute to some of the most influential Rebels, Rockers, Starlets, Icons, and Fashionistas of the past 60 years. Using color, texture, and technique—the tools of crochet design—extremely talented contributors have helped me channel the essence of some of the celebrities who epitomize pop culture. We've translated the soulful spirit of Erykah Badu, the gracefulness of Esther Williams, and the sultry beauty of Dita Von Teese into colorful projects that evoke their unique personalities. Johnny Depp's dark, gypsy-like mystique, Selena Gomez's youthful spark, and Doris Day's girl-next-door goodness are interpreted in

Janis Joplin often wore crocheted vests.

## If pop culture influences everything we do, that includes our craft.

accessories with memorable texture. Inspired by the infectious, free-spiritedness of Drew Barrymore, the rugged charm of Clint Eastwood, and the sophisticated sense of Vera Wang, we used techniques that reflect the charm, charisma, and aesthetic of each.

Much like the personalities who inspired them, the garments in this book range in style from clean and classic to frilly and funky. Even if you're not me— my fashion foundation was established by the characters played by Molly Ringwald and Annie Potts in *Pretty in Pink*—there's a little somethin' for everyone who's got some yarn and ain't afraid to use it.

Are you hooked yet? Well, get ready, because crochet's about to go POP!

June Carter Cash showing off a magnificent dress (and body)!

Michel Euler/Associated Press

Kristie Bull/Graylock.com/Associated Press

James Devaney/WireImage/Getty Images

★ **REBELS** ★

# Dita

Designer: **M.K. Carroll**

The starlets of the '30s and '40s embodied the essence of Hollywood glamour. Today, burlesque stars like Dita Von Teese emulate these sirens of the silver screen. The look—lush fabrics, impeccable accessories, and porcelain make up—has inspired a felted, scalloped clutch, an accessory that proves vintage is eternally vogue.

## HANDBAG BODY

With A and larger hook, ch 68. Turn.

*Row 1*: Ch 1, hdc in 2nd ch from hook and across.

*Row 2*: Ch 1, hdc across.

*Rows 3–48*: Rep Row 2.

Fasten off.

Fold in half vertically, so that rows create vertical lines from top to bottom of bag. Sc sides together, leaving top open. Weave in ends. Tie a knot in the end of the strand of mercerized cotton yarn. With cotton yarn, baste the open ends of the bag together to hold straight while felting.

### Felt

Felt bag in washing machine, placing it in zippered pillowcase if desired. When bag is felted to size, remove basting, tug to shape, and allow to dry completely. If desired, shave with clippers for a more smooth look.

## SCALLOP LACE (MAKE 2)

With B and smaller hook, ch 112.

*Row 1*: Skip 1st ch, sc into rem 111 chs. Turn.

*(continued next page)*

---

**LEVEL: INTERMEDIATE**

### Size
One Size

### Finished Measurements
7½ x 12"/19 x 30cm

### You Will Need
SWTC Karaoke (50% Soysilk, 50% wool; 1.75oz/50g = 109yd/100m): (A) 4 skeins, color Lavender Rose #294; (B) 1 skein, color Black #295—approx 545yd/500m of worsted-weight yarn, (4)

Hooks: 3.75mm/F-5 and 5.5mm/I-9 or size needed to obtain gauge

1–2 yds/1–2m worsted-weight mercerized cotton yarn (for basting edge of bag pre-felting)

Purse frame with sewing holes and loops, 8"/20cm wide

Purse chain, 15"/38cm or desired length

2 jump rings or split rings, 2.5mm in diameter

14 x 17"/36 x 43cm medium-weight fabric to match (B) (for lining)

Yarn needle

Sewing needle

Straight pins

Sewing thread to match (A)

Sewing thread to match (B)

Electric hair clippers (optional, to shave finished bag)

### Stitches Used
Chain (ch)

Single crochet (sc)

Half double crochet (hdc)

Double crochet (dc)

### Gauge
*Take time to check your gauge.*

23 sts = 4"/10cm in hdc using larger hook (after felting)

13 rows = 4"/10cm in hdc using larger hook (after felting)

**Row 2**: Ch 1, sc into 1st sc, ch 2, skip 2 sts, 1 sc in next st, ch 8, skip 3, 1 sc in next st, *ch 5, skip 5 sts, 1 sc in next st, ch 8, skip 3 sts, 1 sc in next st; rep from * to last 3 sts, ch 2, sc in last st, turn.

**Row 3**: Ch 1, 1 sc in 1st st, 16 dc into ch-8 loop of previous row, *1 sc into next ch-5 loop of previous row, 16 dc into next ch-8 loop of previous row; rep from * to last 2 sts, sc in last st (11 scallops made). Fasten off.

## FINISH
Weave in ends. Wash and block, gently tugging scallops into shape. Let dry completely.

## Sew Bag to Frame
Turn bag body inside out. With yarn needle and A, whipstitch together 1¼"/3cm along the side of the top edge. Fasten off and rep on the other side. Turn RS out. Open purse frame completely (so it lies flat). Line up the seam with the hinge of the frame. Tuck edge of bag firmly against the inside edge of the frame, and with sewing needle and matching thread, secure the corners of the bag to the frame with provisional basting sts. With sewing needle and matching thread, use an overcast stitch to stitch the bag to the frame, keeping fabric firmly tucked against the inside edge of the frame: from inside of bag, push needle through below edge of frame; from outside, go through a sewing hole and the fabric; repeat.

## Sew Scallop Lace to Bag
Line up strip of scallop lace with sides of bag and edge of frame. With straight pins, secure the ends of the lace to the corners of the bag, then secure the center scallop to the middle of the top section. Pin top corners of scallop lace in position. With sewing needle and matching thread, stitch the sc edge of the lace into place. When working along the purse frame edge, use the edge of the lace to cover the sewing holes in the purse frame and use the sewing holes to stitch the lace to the frame using a small running stitch. The ch-5 sections can be stitched closed or opened up as desired. Smooth down and pin scallop section of lace into place and stitch down.

Repeat on other side.

## Lining
Fold fabric in half and sew ½"/1cm seams along sides. Turn down and press ½"/1cm hem along top, and sew in place. Tuck into bag so WS are touching. Pin into place and with sewing needle and thread, sew lining to handbag using the sewing holes along the top and whipstitching or slipstitching along the edges that are not along the frame.

## Chain
Using jump rings or split rings, attach chain to loops on handbag frame.

Designer: **John Brinegar**

## Size

S(M, L)

## Finished Measurements

Chest: 36(40, 44)"/91(102, 112)cm
Length: 33(34, 35)"/84(86, 89)cm

## You Will Need

Filatura di Crosa Zara Plus (100%
   wool; 1.75oz/50g = 77yd/70m):
   (A), 17(19, 21) skeins, color Black
   #30; (B), 1 skein, color Charcoal
   #28—approx 1386(1540, 1694)
   yd/1260(1400, 1540)m of worsted-
   weight yarn, **(4)**
Hooks: 3.75mm/F-5 and 5mm/H-8
   or size needed to obtain gauge
15 buttons, 18mm in diameter

## Stitches Used

Chain (ch)
Single crochet (sc)
Half double crochet (hdc)
Slip stitch (sl st)

## Gauge

*Take time to check your gauge.*
15 sc = 4"/10cm using larger hook
17 rows = 4"/10cm in sc using
   larger hook

***Note:*** This garment is meant
   to be fitted.

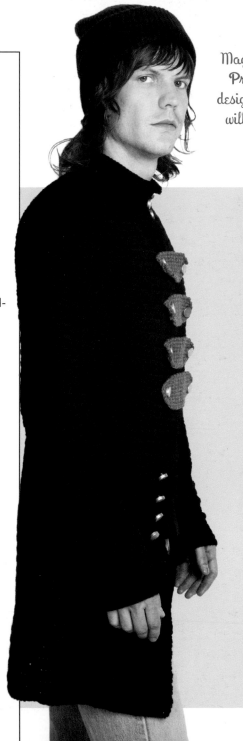

*Magazines like* **NYLON** *and* **GQ** *and TV's*
**Project Runway** *have dudes dying to go
designer. This Marc Jacobs-inspired jacket
will have hipsters and metrosexuals alike
hooked on haute crochet.*

## LEFT FRONT

With larger hook and A, ch 41(47, 53).
Hdc in 3rd ch from hook and in each ch
across [40(46, 52) hdc]. Work even in hdc
for 10"/25cm, ending with a RS row.

*Next row (WS):* Hdc to last 2 sts,
   hdc2tog. Ch 2, turn, skip 1st hdc,
   hdc across. Sc even for 6"/15cm more,
   ending with a RS row.

*Next row (WS):* Sc to last st, work 2 sc in
   same st, ch 2 (counts as hdc), turn; 2
   hdc in same sp, hdc across.

Work even in hdc until piece measures
22½(23, 23½)"/57(58, 60)cm from beg,
ending with a RS row, ch 2, turn.

## SHAPE ARMHOLE

*Next row (WS):* Hdc across to last
   4 sts, turn.

*Next row:* Ch 2, work even to last st,
   ch 2, turn.

*Next row:* Work hdc to last 2 hdc,
   hdc2tog, ch 2, turn.

Work last 2 rows 2(3, 4) times more,
then work even until armhole measures
10½(11, 11½)"/27(28, 29)cm, ending
with a WS row. Ch 2, turn [33(38, 43)
hdc].

## SHAPE NECK

**Next row (RS):** Work 18(19, 20) hdc, 1 sc in next st, ch 1, turn.

**Next row:** Sc in 1st sc, hdc across, ch 2, turn.

**Next row:** Hdc across to last 2 sts, hdc2tog, ch 1, turn.

**Next row:** Sc in 1st sc, hdc across, ch 2, turn.

Work even 2 more rows, fasten off.

## RIGHT FRONT

With larger hook and A, ch 35(38, 41). Work as for Left Front, reversing all shaping. Right Front should mirror Left Front.

## BACK

With larger hook and A, ch 69(75, 81). Hdc in 3rd ch from hook and in each ch across (68[74, 80] hdc). Work even in hdc for 10"/25cm, ch 2, turn. Skip 1st st, hdc to last 2 sts, hdc2tog.

Rep last row once more, then work even in sc for 6"/15cm, ch 1, turn. Work 2 sc in 1st sc, sc to last st, 2 sc in same st, ch 2, turn. Work 2 hdc in 1st st, hdc to last st, 2 hdc in last st.

Work even in hdc until piece measures 22½(23, 23½)"/57(58, 60)cm from beg, ch 1, turn.

## SHAPE ARMHOLE

Sl st over 1st 4 sts, hdc to last 4 sts, turn.

Dec 1 st at each end of next 3(4, 5) rows (61[66, 71] hdc). Work even until piece measures same as for front. Fasten off.

## SLEEVES (MAKE 2)

With larger hook and A, ch 37(39, 42). Sc in 2nd ch from hook and in each ch across (36[38, 41] sc). Ch 1, turn. Work even in sc for 2"/5cm. Change to hdc and inc 1 st at beg and end of every 4th row 22(23, 23) times (80[84, 87] hdc). Work even in hdc until sleeve measures 20½(21, 21½)"/52(53, 55)cm from beg.

## SHAPE CAP

Sl st over 1st 4 sts, ch 2, hdc across to last 4 sts, ch 2, turn. Dec 1 st at beg and end of every row until 26(28, 31) sts remain. Fasten off.

## FINISH

Sew shoulder seams. Set in sleeves, sew sleeve and side seams. Weave in ends.

## COLLAR

With larger hook and A, join yarn with sl st at right neck edge (RS facing). Work even in sc around neck, working through the front loops *only*, ch 1, turn.

**Next row:** 2 sc, ch 2, skip 2 sc, sc to end.

**Next row:** Sc around, working 1 sc in each ch of ch-2 space (buttonhole made).

Work 2 rows even in sc.

Rep last 4 rows twice more, working 1 row even on last repeat.

## BUTTONBANDS (MAKE 4)

With smaller hook and B, ch 5.

**Next row:** Sc in 2nd ch from hook and in each ch across, ch 1, turn (5 sc).

**Next row:** 2 sc in 1st sc, sc to last sc, 2 sc in last ch of prev row, ch 1, turn (7 sc).

**Next row:** Sc in 1st 2 sc, ch 2, skip 2 sc, sc in last 2 sc, ch 1, turn.

**Next row:** 2 sc in 1st sc, sc in each sc across, working 1 sc in each of the ch 2, ending with 2 sc in last sc (9 sc).

Work even for 16 rows.

**Next row:** Ch 1, turn, dec 1 sc over 1st 2 sc, sc to last 2 sts, dec 1 st over those 2 sts, ch 1, turn.

**Next row:** Sc in 1st 2 sc, ch 2, skip 2 sc, sc in last 2 sc, ch 1, turn.

**Next row:** Dec 1 st over 1st 2 sc, 1 sc in each of previous row's ch 2, dec 1 sc over last 2 sts. Ch 1, turn. Work 1 sc in each sc, fasten off.

**Note:** The button bands will curl slightly, due to the tighter gauge at which they are worked. Simply wet-block them and lay them flat to dry. *Do not* stretch them to any specific measurement.

## WAISTBAND BUTTONHOLES

With larger hook and A, with RS facing, join with sl st at the top of the sc section on the Left Front of coat (waist shaping section). *Ch 2, sc in next 4 sts along side, rep from * 3 times more (4 buttonholes made).

Fasten off and attach buttons to corresponding place on Right Front of coat.

Sew 3 buttons opposite buttonholes on collar. Sew buttons for buttonbands on upper portion of coat in 2 columns; fasten buttonbands over buttons.

★ *Sean*

*Designer:* **Drew Emborsky**

18

## Size

One Size

## Finished Measurements

Circumference: 23"/58cm

## You Will Need

Berroco Ultra Alpaca (50% super-
fine alpaca, 50% wool; 3.5oz/100g
= 215yd/198m): 1 skein, color
Charcoal Mix #6289—approx
215yd/198m of worsted-weight
yarn, (4)

Hook: 3.75mm/F-5 or size needed
to obtain gauge

Yarn needle

Stitch markers

## Stitches Used

Chain (ch)

Single crochet (sc)

Double crochet (dc)

Front post double crochet (fpdc)

Back post double crochet (bpdc)

Slip stitch (sl st)

## Gauge

*Take time to check your gauge.*

20 dc = 4"/10cm

10 rows = 4"/10cm

You can tell a lot about
a guy by his headwear.
Fedora: indie hipster.
Trucker cap: trend follower.
Team logo hat: sports fan.
The popularity of hats and
the stereotypes associated
with them may change through
the years, but nothing's sexier
than a man in a driver's cap.
Made in alpaca, it brings
out the best side of even the
baddest of boys.

## CAP

Ch 35, sc into 2nd ch from hook and
into each ch across, turn (34 sc).

**Row 1**: Ch 3, *skip 1 st, dc into next
3 sts, working behind sts just made,
dc in skipped st; rep from * across,
dc in last st, turn.

**Row 2 (RS)**: Ch 1, sc in each st across,
turn.

**Row 3**: Ch 3, *[skip 1 st, dc into next
3 sts, working behind sts just made,
dc in skipped st]** 4 times, ch 2; rep
from * to ** 4 times more, dc in last
st, turn.

**Row 4**: Ch 1, sc across, working 3 sc in
ch-2 sp, turn (37 sc).

**Row 5**: Ch 3, [skip 1 st, dc into next
3 sts, working behind sts just made,
dc in skipped st] 4 times, skip 1 sc,
3 dc in next st, skip 1 sc, [skip 1 st,
dc into next 3 sts, working behind sts
just made, dc in skipped st] 4 times
more, dc in last st, turn.

**Row 6**: Ch 1, sc across, turn.

**Rows 7–36**: Rep Rows 5–6, pm at beg of
Row 36.

**Rows 37–39**: Ch 1, sl st 5, sc to within
last 5 sts of row, sl st 1, turn.

Fasten off.

*(continued next page)*

## BRIM

**Row 1**: With RS facing, join with a sc to 1st st of Row 36, work sc evenly across until you reach the last st of Row 36, working in sl sts where necessary, turn.

**Rows 2–11**: Ch 1, sc in each st across, turn.

At the end of Row 11 do not turn and do not fasten off.

## HEADBAND

**Rnd 1**: Mark next st as beg of rnd, cont to sc evenly around edge of hat, across foundation ch, along other edge of hat, and across brim.

**Rnds 2–3**: Sc around.

**Rnd 4**: Dc around.

**Rnd 5**: *Fpdc, bpdc; rep from * around.

**Rnd 6**: Fpdc around each FP st around, leaving the BP sts unworked; do not join, do not fasten off.

## SIDES

**Row 1**: Ch 3, *fpdc, bpdc, rep from * across, ending with st directly below marker placed at beg of Row 36, turn.

**Rows 2–7**: Work each row in ribbing as established, leaving last 2 sts of each row unworked.

At the end of Row 7 do not turn, work 1 row of sc evenly around hat. Fasten off.

## FINISH

Weave in all ends, block if desired.

*Designer:* **Kelley Deal**

21

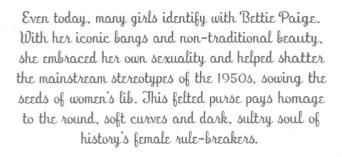

Even today, many girls identify with Bettie Paige. With her iconic bangs and non-traditional beauty, she embraced her own sexuality and helped shatter the mainstream stereotypes of the 1950s, sowing the seeds of women's lib. This felted purse pays homage to the round, soft curves and dark, sultry soul of history's female rule-breakers.

**LEVEL: BEGINNER**

## SMALL VERSION
### Size
One Size

### Finished Measurements
9"/23cm in diameter

### You Will Need
Brown Sheep Nature Spun Worsted (100% wool; 3.5oz/100g = 245yd/224m): (A), 1 skein, color roasted coffee #N98W—approx 245yd/224m of worsted-weight yarn, (4)

Classic Elite La Gran (76.5% mohair, 17.5% wool, 6% nylon; 1.48oz/42g = 90yd/82m): (B), 1 skein, color black #06513—approx 90yd/82m of worsted-weight yarn, (4)

Hooks: 4mm/G-6 and 5.5mm/I-9 or size needed to obtain gauge

8"/20 cm metal ring (spray painted black, if desired)

Yarn needle

3 clip rings for ¼"/6mm rod, black 12"/30cm black wire, 26 gauge

Small assortment of black beads, beading needle, and beading thread

### Stitches Used
Chain (ch)
Single crochet (sc)
Double crochet (dc)
Slip stitch (sl st)

### Gauge
*Take time to check your gauge.*
11 dc = 4"/10cm with larger hook and yarn held doubled
5 rows = 4"/10cm with larger hook and yarn held doubled

## BAG SIDES (MAKE 2)
With one strand of each yarn held together:

*Row 1*: Ch 4, join with sl st in 1st ch to form ring, ch 2, 5 dc in ring, ch 2 and turn work (6 dc).

*Row 2*: Dc in same st as ch 2, 2 dc in each dc, ch 2, turn (12 dc).

*Row 3*: Dc in same st as ch 2, * dc in next dc, 2 dc in next dc **, rep from * to ** around, ch 2, turn (18 dc).

*Row 4*: Dc in same st as ch 2, * dc in next 2 dc, 2 dc in next dc **, rep from * to ** around, ch 2, turn (24 dc).

*Row 5*: Dc in same st as ch 2, * dc in next 3 dc, 2 dc in next dc **, rep from * to ** around, ch 2, turn (30 dc).

*Row 6*: Dc in same st as ch 2, * dc in next 4 dc, 2 dc in next dc **, rep from * to ** around, ch 2, turn (36 dc).

*Row 7*: Dc in same st as ch 2, * dc in next 5 dc, 2 dc in next dc **, rep from * to ** around, ch 2, turn (42 dc).

*Row 8*: Dc in same st as ch 2, * dc in next 6 dc, 2 dc in next dc **, rep from * to ** around, ch 2, turn (48 dc).

*Row 9*: Dc in same st as ch 2, * dc in next 7 dc, 2 dc in next dc **, rep from * to ** around (54 dc).

## FINISH

Align the bag sides, sc curved edges together with one strand of each yarn held together, leaving straight side open. This will be the bag opening.

## Top Edge Trim

With one strand of each yarn held together and 5.5mm crochet hook:

*Rnd 1*: Sl st into top of bag, ch 2, place 61 dc evenly around top edge of bag, sl st into beginning ch 2 (62 dc).

*Rnd 2*: Ch 2, dc around, join with sl st (62 dc).

Fasten off. Weave in ends.

## Felt and Block

Felt bag in washing machine, placing it in zippered pillowcase if desired. Slide metal ring into freshly felted bag. Tug and pull at the bag to get a snug fit. If the bag is too loose, felt it again until the fit feels snug. Lay flat to dry.

## Assemble

With single strand of A and 4mm hook, sc 41 st around metal ring. Find the bottom of the bag and the 21st st along the metal ring. Slide ring into bag so that the 21st st is at the center of the bottom of the bag. Using yarn needle and 8"/20cm piece of A, tack the 21st st along metal ring to the bottom of the bag. This is the bottom tack. Tack top left and top right edges of the bag in the same manner; work blindly from the inside of the bag so that your work will be hidden. These tack points might feel a bit clumsy to do; be sure to hide your ends. Continue tacking in this manner along the ring until you have approximately 9 tack points. Weave in ends.

## Decorative Trim

Wire together the 3 drapery rings. Attach drapery rings to bag using a beaded string of desired length.

## LARGE VERSION

### Size

One Size

### Finished Measurements

Diameter: 15"/38cm

### You Will Need

Reynolds Lite Lopi (100% wool; 1.75oz/50g = 109yd/100m): (A), 2 skeins, color ochre or gold heather—approx 218yd/200m of worsted-weight yarn, (4)

Vimar Maggiore Dalia (50% wool, 50% acrylic; 1.75oz/50g = 19yd/17m): (B), 1 skein—approx 19yd/17m of super bulky-weight yarn, (6)

Hooks: 4mm/G-6, 5.5mm/I-9, and 8mm/L-11 or size needed to obtain gauge

14"/36cm metal ring

Yarn needle

Sewing needle and thread

Glue gun to attach trim

### Stitches Used

Chain (ch)

Single crochet (sc)

Double crochet (dc)

Slip stitch (sl st)

### Gauge

*Take time to check your gauge.*

11 dc = 4"/10cm using 5.5mm hook

6 rows = 4"/10cm using 5.5mm hook

## BAG SIDES (MAKE 2)

*Note:* Though sides are started with a ring, work is completed in rows to form a half circle.

***Row 1***: With 5.5mm hook and A, ch 4, join with sl st in 1st ch to form ring; ch 2, 5 dc in ring, ch 2 and turn work (6 dc).

***Row 2***: Dc in same st as ch 2, 2 dc in each dc, ch 2, turn (12 dc).

***Row 3***: Dc in same st as ch 2, * dc in next dc, 2 dc in next dc **, rep from * to ** around, ch 2, turn (18 dc).

***Row 4***: Dc in same st as ch 2, * dc in next 2 dc, 2 dc in next dc **, rep from * to ** around, ch 2, turn (24 dc).

***Row 5***: Dc in same st as ch 2, * dc in next 3 dc, 2 dc in next dc **, rep from * to ** around, ch 2, turn (30 dc).

***Row 6***: Dc in same st as ch 2, * dc in next 4 dc, 2 dc in next dc **, rep from * to ** around, ch 2, turn (36 dc).

***Row 7***: Dc in same st as ch 2, * dc in next 5 dc, 2 dc in next dc **, rep from * to ** around, ch 2, turn (42 dc).

***Row 8***: Dc in same st as ch 2, * dc in next 6 dc, 2 dc in next dc **, rep from * to ** around, ch 2, turn (48 dc).

**Row 9**: Dc in same st as ch 2, * dc in next 7 dc, 2 dc in next dc **, rep from * to ** around, ch 2, turn (54 dc).

**Row 10**: Dc in same st as ch 2, * dc in next 8 dc, 2 dc in next dc **, rep from * to ** around, ch 2, turn (60 dc).

**Row 11**: Dc in same st as ch 2, * dc in next 9 dc, 2 dc in next dc **, rep from * to ** around, ch 2, turn (66 dc).

**Row 12**: Dc in same st as ch 2, * dc in next 10 dc, 2 dc in next dc **, rep from * to ** around, ch 2, turn (72 dc).

**Row 13**: Dc in same st as ch 2, * dc in next 11 dc, 2 dc in next dc **, rep from * to ** around, ch 2, turn (78 dc).

**Row 14**: Dc in same st as ch 2, * dc in next 12 dc, 2 dc in next dc **, rep from * to ** around, ch 2, turn (84 dc).

**Row 15**: Dc in same st as ch 2, * dc in next 13 dc, 2 dc in next dc **, rep from * to ** around, ch 2, turn (90 dc).

**Row 16**: Dc in same st as ch 2, * dc in next 14 dc, 2 dc in next dc **, rep from * to ** around (96 dc).

## FINISH

Align the bag sides, sc curved edges together, leaving straight side open. This will be the bag opening.

## Top Edge Trim

With 5.5mm crochet hook and A:

**Rnd 1**: Sl st into top of bag, ch 2, work 99 dc evenly around top edge of bag, sl st into beginning ch 2 (100 dc).

**Rnd 2**: Ch 2, dc2tog 6 times evenly around edge, sl st into beginning ch 2 (94 dc).

**Rnds 3–5**: Ch 2, dc2tog 4 times evenly around edge, sl st into beginning ch 2 (90 dc).

Fasten off. Weave in ends.

## Felt and Block

Follow your preferred method of felting. Slide metal ring into freshly felted bag. Tug and pull at the bag to get a snug fit. If the bag is too loose, felt it again until the fit feels snug. Lay flat to dry.

## Assemble

With 4mm hook and A, sc 81 sts around metal ring. Find the bottom of the bag and the 41st st along the metal ring. Slide ring into bag so that the 41st st is at the center of the bottom of the bag. Using yarn needle and length of corresponding yarn, tack the 41st st along metal ring to the bottom of the bag. This is the bottom tack. Tack top left and top right edges of the bag in the same manner; work blindly from the inside of the bag so that your work will be hidden. These tack points might feel a bit clumsy to do; be sure to hide your ends. Continue tacking in this manner in approx 2"/5cm intervals. Finish off. Weave in ends.

## Decorative Trim

With 8mm crochet hook and B, ch 63, turn, dc in 3rd ch from hook and across (62 dc).

Finish off. Weave in ends.

Glue or sew trim to top edge of bag.

REBELS ★ David

Designer: **Vickie Howell**

*The famous progeny of A-listers—tykes like Maddox Jolie-Pitt or David Banda Ritchie—are small but mighty, and not afraid to dress accordingly. A camo peacoat will keep your little rascal looking tough but feeling cozy.*

**LEVEL: BEGINNER**

## Sizes
Child's 2(4, 6)

## Finished Measurements
Chest: 24(27, 28)"/61(69, 71)cm
Length: 13½(14½, 15½)"/34 (37, 39)cm

## You Will Need
Lorna's Laces Shepherd Worsted (100% superwash wool; 4oz/113g = 225yd/205m): (A), 3(4, 5) skeins, color Camouflage—approx 675(900, 1125)yd/615(820, 1025)m of worsted-weight yarn, (4)

SWTC Vickie Howell Collection Rock (40% Soysilk, 30% fine wool, 30% hemp; 1.75oz/50g = 109yd/100m): (B), 1 skein, color Billy #755—approx 109yd/100m of worsted-weight yarn, (4)

Hook: 5.5mm/I-9 or size needed to obtain gauge
Yarn needle
6 buttons, 1"/3cm in diameter
Sewing needle and thread

## Stitches Used
Chain (ch)
Single crochet (sc)
Half double crochet (hdc)
Double crochet (dc)
Slip stitch (sl st)

## Gauge
*Take time to check your gauge.*
15 sc = 4"/10cm
9 rows = 4"/10cm

## BACK
With A, ch 45(50, 53).

*Row 1*: Sc in 2nd ch from hook and in every ch to end. Turn.

*Row 2*: Ch 1 (counts as 1st sc, here and throughout), sc to end. Turn.

Rep Row 2.

*Next row*: Ch 3, dc to end. Turn.

Rep last row.

*Next row*: Ch 1, sc across. Turn.

Rep last row until piece measures 9(9½, 10)"/23(24, 25)cm.

## SHAPE ARMHOLE
*Next row*: Ch 1, sc2tog (the base of ch 1 counts as 1st sc) twice, ch 1, sc to end. Turn.

Rep last row once more [41(46, 49) sc].

*Next row*: Ch 1, sc to end.

Rep last row until piece measures 13¼(14¼, 15¼)"/34(36, 39)cm.

## SHAPE SHOULDER
*Next row (RS)*: Ch 1, 2 sc, 3 hdc, 4 dc, 21(26, 29) sc, 4 dc, 3 hdc, 3 sc (this will create sloped shoulders). Fasten off.

*(continued next page)*

## RIGHT FRONT

With A, ch 33(37, 39).

*Row 1*: Sc in next st and in every ch to end. Turn.

*Row 2*: Ch 1, sc to end. Turn.

Rep Row 2.

*Next row*: Ch 3, dc to end. Turn.

Rep last row.

*Next row*: Ch 1, sc to end. Turn.

Rep last row until piece measures 9(9½, 10)"/23(24, 25)cm.

### SHAPE ARMHOLE

*Next row*: Ch 1, sc2tog twice, sc to end.

*Next row*: Ch 1, sc to end. Turn.

Rep last row until piece measures 13¼(14¼, 15¼)"/34(36, 39)cm, ending with a RS row.

### SHAPE NECK/SHOULDER

*Next row (WS)*: Ch 1, 9 sc. Turn.

*Next row*: Ch 3, 3 dc, 3 hdc, 3 sc. Fasten off.

### LEFT FRONT

With A, ch 27(30, 32).

*Row 1*: Sc in next st and in every ch to end. Turn.

*Row 2*: Ch 1, sc to end. Turn.

Rep Row 2.

*Next row*: Ch 3, dc to end. Turn.

Rep last row.

*Next row*: Ch 1, sc to end. Turn.

Rep last row until piece measures 4(4½, 5)"/10(11, 13)cm, ending with a WS row.

### BUTTONHOLE ROWS

*Buttonhole Row 1 (RS)*: Ch 1, sc in next 13(16, 18) sts, ch 4, skip 3, sc in next 4 sts, ch 4, skip 3, sc to end.

*Buttonhole Row 2*: Ch 1, sc to 1st ch-4 sp, 3 sc in ch-4 sp, sc in next 4 sts, 3 sc in next ch-4 sp, sc to end.

*Next row*: Ch 1, sc to end. Turn.

Rep last row until piece measures 7½(8, 8½)"/19(20, 22)cm, ending with a WS row.

Rep Buttonhole rows.

*Next row*: Ch 1, sc to end. Turn.

Rep last row until piece measures 9(9½, 10)"/23(24, 25)cm, ending with a WS row.

### SHAPE ARMHOLE

*Next row*: Ch 1, sc2tog twice, sc to end. Turn.

*Next row*: Ch 1, sc to end. Turn.

Rep last row until piece measures 11(12, 13)"/28(30, 33)cm, ending with a WS row.

Rep Buttonhole rows.

*Next row*: Ch 1, sc to end. Turn.

Rep last row until piece measures 13¼(14¼, 15¼)"/34(36, 39)cm, ending with a RS row.

## SHAPE NECK/SHOULDER

*Next row (WS)*: 15 sl sts, ch 1, sc to end. Turn.

*Next row*: Ch 3, 3 dc, 3 hdc, 3 sc. Fasten off.

## COLLAR

With A, ch 39(43, 47).

*Next row*: Sc in 2nd ch from hook and in every ch to end. Turn.

*Next row*: Ch 1, sc to end. Turn.

*Next row*: Ch 1, sc in base of ch, sc to last st, 2 sc in same st [41(45, 49) sc]. Turn.

*Next row*: Ch 1, sc to end. Turn.

Rep last 2 rows twice [45(49, 53) sc].

Next row: Ch 2, hdc to end. Fasten off.

## SLEEVES (MAKE 2)

With A, ch 31(35, 39).

*Row 1*: Sc in next st and to end. Turn.

*Row 2*: Ch 1, sc to end. Turn.

Rep Row 2 three times more.

*Next (inc) row*: Ch 1, sc in base of ch, sc to last st, 2 sc in same st [33(37, 41) sc]. Turn.

Cont as established, working 5 rows in straight sc and 1 inc row, 6 times more [45(49, 53) sc].

*Next row*: Ch 1, sc to end. Turn.

Rep last row until sleeve measures 8(10, 11)"/20(25, 28)cm.

*Next row*: Ch 1, sc2tog, sc to last 2 sts, sc2tog [43(47, 51) sc]. Turn.

Rep last row twice more [39(43, 47) sc].

*Next row*: Ch 1, sc2tog twice, sc to last 4 sts, sc2tog twice [35(39, 43) sc]. Turn.

*Next row*: Ch 1, sc2tog, sc to last 2 sts, sc2tog [33(37, 41) sc]. Turn.

*Next row*: 6 sl sts, ch 1, sc to last 6 sts, 6 sl sts. Fasten off.

## FAUX POCKETS (MAKE 2)

With A, ch 12.

*Row 1*: Sc in 2nd ch from hook and to end. Turn.

*Row 2*: Ch 1, sc to end. Turn.

Rep Row 2 twice more. Fasten off.

## FINISH

Seam together using preferred method, beginning with the shoulders, then the sleeves and the sides. Attach collar, taking care to make sure it's centered along the neckline.

Using sewing needle and thread, sew on buttons to Right Front to correspond with buttonhole placement.

Using yarn needle, double strand of B, and a running stitch, embroider detailing on sleeves, collar, and pockets as shown in photo.

★ *Johnny*

Designer: **Vickie Howell**

## Size
Men's One Size Fits All

## Finished Measurements
Wrist Warmer: Fits up to 8"/20cm wrist

Scarf: 15 x 90"/38 x 229cm

## You Will Need
SWTC Vickie Howell Collection Rock (40% Soysilk, 30% fine wool, 30% hemp; 1.75oz/50g = 109yd/100m): (A), 2 skeins, color Thom #759; (B), 2 skeins color Trent #760— approx 436yd/400m of worsted-weight yarn, **(4)**

Hook: 5mm/H-8 or size needed to obtain gauge

Yarn needle

### *Scarf Only*
15 x 90"/38 x 229cm piece of jersey fabric

Coordinating thread

Sewing needle

## Stitches Used
Chain (ch)

Single crochet (sc)

## Gauge
*Take time to check your gauge.*

16 sc = 4"/10cm

14 rows = 4"/10cm

*Whether playing an undercover cop, a high-rolling drug dealer, or a crazy candy maker, Johnny Depp always looks good. It's his own gypsy-writer style, though, that most turns heads and makes hearts throb.*

## WRIST WARMERS

### (MAKE 2)
With A, ch 36.

*Row 1*: Sc in 2nd chain from hook and to end. Turn.

*Row 2*: Ch 1, sc to end. Turn.

*Rows 3–12*: Rep Row 2.

*Row 13 (RS)*: Ch 1, 17 sc (leaving rest of row unworked, forming slit), ch 18. Turn.

*Row 14*: Sc in 2nd ch from hook and to end.

*Row 15*: Switch to B. Ch 1, sc to end. Turn.

*Row 16*: Rep Row 2.

*Row 17*: Switch back to A. Ch 1, sc to end. Turn.

*Rows 18–28*: Rep Row 2. Fasten off.

### FINISH
Weave in ends.

With yarn needle and B, stitch a zigzag formation at slit, with the sts gradually becoming longer closer to the top edge.

Fold piece in half lengthwise and seam up side.

## SCARF

### WIDE STRIPE
With B, ch 350.

*Row 1*: Sc in 2nd ch from hook and to end. Turn.

*Row 2*: Ch 1, sc to end. Turn.

Rep Row 2 two times more. Fasten off.

### SKINNY STRIPE
With B, ch 350.

*Row 1*: Sc in 2nd ch from hook and to end. Turn.

*Row 2*: Ch 1, sc to end. Fasten off.

### FINISH
Weave in ends. Pin or tape down fabric scarf on a flat surface so it's taut. Using a sewing needle and coordinating thread, hand-tack crocheted stripes onto fabric as desired.

★ ICONS ★

Designer: **Jennifer Fletcher**

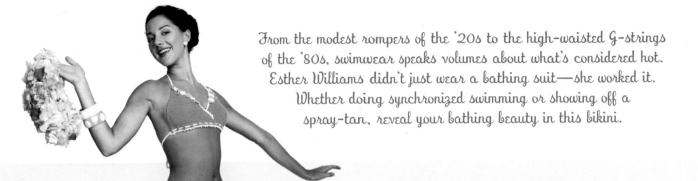

From the modest rompers of the '20s to the high-waisted G-strings of the '80s, swimwear speaks volumes about what's considered hot. Esther Williams didn't just wear a bathing suit—she worked it. Whether doing synchronized swimming or showing off a spray-tan, reveal your bathing beauty in this bikini.

**LEVEL: INTERMEDIATE**

## Size

Top (bust): Small/Medium (33–37"/84–94cm) and Large (38–40"/97–102cm)

Bottom (hips): Small (34–35"/ 86–89cm), Medium (36–37"/ 91–94cm), and Large (38–40"/ 97–102cm)

## Finished Measurements

Top (not including ties): 14½(15½)"/37(39)cm wide

Bottom: 31½(32½, 33½)"/80(83, 85) cm at hips

## You Will Need

Cascade Fixation (98.3% cotton, 1.7% elastic; 1.75oz/50g = 100yd/91m): (A), 4(5) balls, color Turquoise #2706; (B), 1 ball, color White #8001—approx 500(600)yd/455(546)m of DK-weight yarn, ③.
Additional colors for decoration: 1 ball each Light Green #5184, Apricot #4545, and Yellow #1300 (optional)

Hooks: 2mm/4 steel, 2.75mm/C-2, and 3.25mm/D-3 or size needed to obtain gauge

Yarn needle

1½ yds/137cm waistband elastic, ¼"/6mm wide (optional)

Sewing needle and thread (optional)

## Stitches Used

Chain (ch)

Single crochet (sc)

Half double crochet (hdc)

Double crochet (dc)

Treble crochet (tr)

Slip stitch (sl st)

## Gauge

*Take time to check your gauge.*

26 sc = 4"/10cm using 2.75mm hook

28 rows = 4"/10cm using 2.75mm hook

## BIKINI TOP

### RIGHT CUP

With A and 2.75mm hook, starting from side of cup:

*Row 1*: Ch 25(28), sc in 2nd ch from hook, sc in each ch across, ch 1, turn, [24(27) sc].

*Row 2*: Sc in each sc across, ch 1, turn.

*Row 3*: Sc2tog over 1st and 2nd sc, sc in each sc across, ch 1, turn [23(26) sc].

*Rows 4–6*: Sc in each sc across, ch 1, turn.

*Row 7*: Rep Row 3 [22(25) sc].

*Rows 8–14*: Sc in each sc across, ch 1, turn.

*Row 15*: Rep Row 3 [21(24) sc].

*Row 16*: Sc in each sc across, ch 16, turn.

*Row 17*: Sc in 2nd ch from hook, sc in next 14 ch, sc in next sc, sc in each sc across, ch 1, turn [36(39) sc].

*Row 18*: Sc in each sc across, ch 1, turn.

*Row 19*: 2 sc in 1st sc, sc in each sc across, ch 1, turn [37(40) sc].

**Pattern through Row 33:**

*Even rows*: Rep Row 18.

*Odd rows*: Rep Row 19 [44(47) sc].

*Row 34*: Sc across to last st, 2 sc in last sc, ch 1, turn [45(48) sc].

*Row 35*: Rep Row 19 [46(49) sc].

*Row 36*: Rep Row 34 [47(50) sc].

*Row 37*: Rep Row 19 [48(51) sc].

*Row 38*: Rep Row 34, fasten off [49(52) sc].

## LEFT CUP

With A and 2.75mm hook, starting from side of cup:

*Row 1*: Ch 25(28), sc in 2nd ch from hook, sc in each ch across, ch 1, turn [24(27) sc].

*Row 2*: Sc in each sc across, ch 1, turn.

*Row 3*: Sc across to last 2 sts, sc2tog over last 2 sc, ch 1, turn [23(26) sc].

*Rows 4–6*: Rep Row 2.

*Row 7*: Rep Row 3 [22(25) sc].

*Rows 8–14*: Rep Row 2.

*Row 15*: Rep Row 3 [21(24) sc].

*Row 16*: Sc in each sc across, fasten off.

Join yarn to *beginning* of Row 16 with sl st, ch 16.

*Row 17*: Sc in 2nd ch from hook, sc in next 14 ch, skip sl st but sc in that sc, sc in each sc across, ch 1, turn [36(39) sc].

*Row 18*: Sc in each sc across, ch 1, turn.

*Row 19*: 2 sc in 1st sc, sc in each sc across, ch 1, turn [37(40) sc].

**Pattern through Row 33:**

*Even rows*: Rep Row 18.

*Odd rows*: Rep Row 19 [44(47) sc].

*Row 34*: Sc across to last st, 2 sc in last sc, ch 1, turn [45(48) sc].

*Row 35*: Rep Row 19 [46(49) sc].

*Row 36*: Rep Row 34 [47(50) sc].

*Row 37*: Rep Row 19 [48(51) sc].

*Row 38*: Rep Row 34, fasten off [49(52) sc].

Sew darts starting from bottom edge with mattress st. Lightly steam cups. Use a tailor's ham or a rounded surface (such as a balled-up sock or tennis ball covered with fabric) to steam dart.

## OUTSIDE EDGE TRIM

*The following indicates three sides of cups: bottom edge (dart), outside edge (shorter side), and inside edge (longer side).*

With A, start at top corner of right cup and sc in each sc along outside edge until midway, then work sc2tog over 2 sts every 4 sts. For left cup, work sc2tog over 2 sts every 4 sts, until midway, and then cont with sc along edge until the end, fasten off.

## PICOT TRIM ON INSIDE EDGES

With B, start with inside corner of right cup:

Sc in next 2 sc, *sc in next sc, ch 3, sl st in 3rd ch from hook, sc in next 2 sc on edge; rep from * across (incl end of outside edge trim), fasten off. Rep for left cup.

Overlap inside corner of left cup and inside corner of right cup 2½"/6cm and hand sew with A along inside edges, making sts as invisible as possible.

## BAND (BOTTOM OF BIKINI TOP)

With A, join yarn with sl st to bottom edge of top (into outside edge trim).

*Row 1*: Sc in each sc across, ch 1, turn.

*Large only*: Rep Row 1.

*Row 2*: Sc in each sc across, ch 4, turn.

*Row 3*: Tr in each sc across, ch 1, turn.

*Row 4*: Sc in each tr across, fasten off.

## PICOT TRIM

With B, join yarn to bottom end of top (RS). *Sc, ch 3, sl st in 3rd ch from hook, sc in next 3 sc; rep from * across band, ending with a picot and a sc in the last 2 sts (if you are off by a couple of sts, it's okay to fudge it), fasten off.

## NECK TIES (MAKE 2)

With B, ch 130(150), hdc in 3rd ch from hook, hdc in each ch across, fasten off.

## BOTTOM TIE

With B, ch 280(310), hdc in 3rd ch from hook, hdc in each ch across, fasten off.

# BOTTOM

## BRIEFS FRONT

*Row 1*: With A and 2.75mm hook, ch 18, sc in 2nd ch from hook, sc in each ch across, ch 1, turn (17 sc).

*(continued next page)*

**Rows 2–12**: Sc in each sc across, ch 1, turn.

**Row 13**: 2 sc in 1st sc, sc across to last st, 2 sc in last sc, ch 1, turn (19 sc).

**Row 14**: Rep Row 13 (21 sc).

**Row 15**: Rep Row 2.

**Row 16**: Rep Row 13 (23 sc).

**Row 17**: Rep Row 2.

**Rows 18–20**: Rep Row 13 (29 sc).

**Row 21**: Rep Row 2.

**Rows 22–23**: Rep Row 13 (33 sc).

**Row 24**: 2 sc in 1st sc, sc across to last st, 2 sc in last sc, ch 35(36, 38) (35 sc, not including chain).

**Row 25**: Sc in 2nd ch from hook, sc in each ch across, sc in each sc across; inc 34(36, 37) sts as follows: make 1 sc in side bar of last sc. Make another sc in side of sc you just made, continue 32 more sc, ch 1, turn [103(106, 109) sc].

**Row 26**: Sc in each sc across, ch 1, turn.

**Row 27**: Sc in next 50(51, 53) sc, sc-2tog, sc in each sc across, ch 1, turn [102(105, 108) sc].

**Row 28**: Sc in next 42(43, 45) sc, sc2tog, sc next 14 sc, sc2tog, sc in each sc across, ch 1, turn [100(103, 106) sc].

**Rows 29–40**: Sc in each sc across, ch 1, turn.

**Row 41**: Sc in each sc across, ch 2, turn.

**Rows 42–43**: Dc in each sc across, ch 2, turn.

*Medium only*: Rep Row 42 two times more.

*Large only*: Rep Row 42 four times more.

**Row 44**: Dc in next 26(27, 29) dc, 1 dec dc in next 2 dc, dc in next 42 dc, 1 dec dc in next 2 dc, dc in each dc across, ch 2, turn [98(101, 104) dc].

**Row 45**: Dc in next 16(17, 19) dc, 1 dec dc in next 2 dc, dc in next 60 dc, 1 dec dc in next 2 dc, dc in each dc across, ch 2, turn [96(99, 102) dc].

**Row 46**: Dc in next 9(11, 12) dc, hdc in next 8 dc, sc in next 15 dc, sc2tog in next 2 dc, sc in next 12 dc, sc2tog in next 2 dc, sc in next 12 dc, sc2tog in next 2 dc, sc in next 15 dc, hdc in next 8 dc, dc in next 10(11, 13) dc, fasten off [93(96, 99) sts].

## BRIEFS BACK

**Row 1**: Ch 18, sc in 2nd ch from hook, sc in each ch across, ch 1, turn (17 sc).

**Rows 2–5**: Sc in each sc across, ch 1, turn.

**Rows 6–7**: 2 sc in 1st sc, sc in each sc across to last st, 2 sc in last sc, ch 1, turn (21 sc).

**Rows 8–9**: Rep Row 2.

### Pattern through Row 16:

**Even rows**: Rep Row 6.

**Odd rows**: Rep Row 2 (29 sc).

**Rows 17–19**: Rep Row 6 (35 sc).

**Row 20**: Rep Row 2.

**Row 21**: Rep Row 6 (37 sc).

**Row 22**: Rep Row 2.

**Rows 23–26**: Rep Row 6 (45 sc).

**Row 27**: 2 sc in 1st sc, sc in each sc across to last st, 2 sc in last sc, ch 3, turn (47 sc).

**Row 28**: Sc in 2nd ch from hook, sc in next ch, sc in each sc across to end; inc 2 sc: make sc in side bar of last sc. Make another sc in side of sc just made (51 sc).

**Rows 29–35**: Rep Row 6 (65 sc).

**Row 36**: 2 sc in 1st sc, sc across to last st, 2 sc in last sc, ch 19(20, 22), turn (67 sc, not including chain).

**Row 37**: Sc in 2nd ch from hook, sc in next 17(17, 20) ch, sc in each sc across; inc end of row by 18(20, 21) sc (as at end of row 28), ch 1, turn [103(106, 109) sc].

**Row 38**: Rep Row 2.

**Row 39**: Sc in next 50(51, 53) sc, sc2tog, sc in each sc across, ch 1, turn [102(105, 108) sc].

**Rows 40–52**: Rep Row 2.

**Row 53**: Sc in next 42(43, 45) sc, sc2tog, sc in next 14 sc, sc2tog, sc in each sc across, ch 2, turn [100(103, 106) sc].

**Rows 54–56**: Dc in each sc across, ch 2, turn.

*Medium only*: Rep Row 54 two times more.

*Large only*: Rep Row 54 four times more.

**Row 57**: Dc in next 34(36, 37) dc, 1 dec dc over 2 dc, dc in next 26 dc, dc in each dc across, ch 2, turn [98(101, 104) dc].

**Row 58**: Dc in next 29(30, 32) dc, 1 dec dc over 2 dc, dc in next 16 dc, 1 dec dc over 2 dc, dc in next 16 dc, 1 dec dc over 2 dc, dc in each dc across, fasten off [95(98, 101) dc].

Sew side seams together with yarn needle and matching yarn. Do the same for crotch seams. Sc around leg openings.

Waist opening now has 188(194, 200) sts.

## WAISTBAND

*Small only*: Rnd 1: Start at right side seam, join A with sl st, sc in same st as sl st, sc in next 16 sts, sc2tog over 2 sts, *sc in next 17 sts, sc2tog in next 2 sts; rep from * around 3 times more, **sc in next 29 sts, sc2tog in next 2 sts; rep from ** around, join (to back loop only), ch 1 (180 sc).

*Medium and Large only*: Rnd 1: Start at right side seam, join A with sl st, sc in same st as sl st, sc in next 21(17) sts, sc2tog over 2 sts, *sc in next 22(18) sts, sc2tog in next 2 sts; rep from * around, *(for Medium, sc in last 2 sts)*, join (to BL only), ch 1 [186(190) sc].

Work *in BL only* for the following rnd:

*Small and Medium only*: Rnd 2: *Sc in next 18(29) sc, sc2tog; rep from * around, join (both loops), ch 1 [171(180) sc].

*Large only*: Rnd 2: sc2tog, *sc in next 45 sc, 1 sc2tog; rep from * around, join (186).

Place st marker in a FL near side seam (to be used later).

*Large only*: Sc in each sc around, join, ch 1.

*(continued next page)*

**All sizes:**

*Rnd 3*: Sc in each sc around, join, ch 4.

*Rnd 4*: Tr in each sc around, join, ch 1.

*Rnd 5*: Sc in each tr around, join, fasten off.

## PICOT TRIM

Join B at one side seam. *Sc, ch 3, sl st in 3rd ch from hook, sc in next 3 sc; rep from * around, fasten off.

## WAIST TIE

With B, ch 260(265, 270), hdc in 3rd ch from hook, hdc in each ch across, fasten off.

## SKIRT

Turn briefs upside down, crotch pointed away. Skirt will be made from the waist down.

With A at marked st, using 3.25mm hook:

*Rnd 1*: *(In FL only for this rnd)* join yarn with sl st, ch 3, dc in next sc, ch 2, *dc in next 2 sc, ch 2; rep from * around, join in both loops, fasten off.

*Rounds 2–5*: Join yarn with sl st in ch-2 sp, ch 3, dc in same ch-2 sp, ch 2, *2 dc in next ch-2 sp, ch 2; rep from * around, fasten off for Small at end of Rnd 5.

*Medium only*: Rep Rnd 2 two times more, fasten off.

*Large only*: Rep Rnd 2 four times more, fasten off.

*Rows worked for slits*: Determine placement for two front slits—directly below hipbone or 2(2¼, 2½)"/5(6, 6)cm from side seams. Use st markers in ch-2 sps. The sts between st markers in front will be referred to as "skirt front."

## SKIRT FRONT

Starting at one marked end:

*Row 1*: Join A with sl st and ch 3 in marked ch-2 sp. Dc in same ch-2 sp, ch 2, *3 dc in next ch-2 sp, ch 2; rep from * across, 2 dc in last (marked) ch-2 sp, ch 3, turn.

*Row 2*: *3 dc in ch-2 sp, ch 2; rep from * across, 3 dc in last ch-2 sp, dc in t-ch, ch 3, turn.

*Row 3*: Dc in sp between last t-ch and dc, ch 2, *3 dc in ch-2 sp, ch 2; rep from * across, dc in sp between last dc and t-ch, dc in t-ch, ch 3, turn.

*Row 4*: Rep Row 2.

*Row 5*: Rep Row 3.

*Row 6*: Rep Row 2.

*Large only*: Rep Row 3 and Row 2 one more time.

*Last row*: Sc into each st and 2 sc in each ch-2 sp across, fasten off.

## SKIRT BACK

Follow directions for Skirt Front, working sts between st markers on back of brief.

## FLOWERS, LEAVES, AND TENDRILS (OPTIONAL)

Double-Petal Flower (Make 2 in Apricot)

*Rnd 1*: With 2mm hook, ch 4, join to make a ring, ch 1, 5 sc into center of ring, join.

*Rnd 2*: *Ch 3, hdc in 2nd ch from hook, sc in next ch, sl st into FL only of next sc on ring; rep from * 4 times more, making last sl st into BL of 1st petal (5 small petals).

*Rnd 3*: *Ch 6, hdc in 3rd ch from hook, dc in next 2 ch, hdc in ch, sl st in BL of next sc on ring; rep from * 4 times more, making last sl st into base of 1st back petal made (5 large petals).

## MEDIUM FLOWER

(Make 4[6] Apricot, 3 White with Yellow centers)

*Rnd 1*: With 2mm hook and yellow, ch 4, join to make a ring, ch 1, 5 sc into center of ring, join, fasten off.

*Rnd 2*: With White, *ch 4, sc in 2nd ch from hook, hdc in next 2 ch, sl st into next sc on ring; rep from * 4 times more, join in base of 1st petal, fasten off (5 petals).

(For Apricot, make both rnds in same color—do not fasten off at end of Rnd 1).

## SMALL FLOWER

(Make 3 White with Yellow centers)

*Rnd 1*: With 2mm hook and yellow, ch 4, join to make a ring, ch 1, 4 sc into center of ring, join, fasten off.

*Rnd 2*: With White, *ch 3, hdc in 2nd ch from hook, sc in next ch, sl st into next sc on ring; rep from * 3 times more, join in base of 1st petal, fasten off (4 petals).

## TENDRILS

(Make 4 in Light Green)

With 2mm hook, ch 25, fasten off. Pull and twist chain into a spiral. Shape will hold.

## LARGE LEAF

(Make 4 in Light Green)

With 2mm hook, ch 9, sc in 2nd ch from hook, dc in next 3 ch, sc in next 2 ch, sl st in next ch, 2 sl st in last ch; working a round to other side of chain: sl st in next ch, sc in next 2 ch, dc in next 3 ch, sc in last ch, fasten off.

## SMALL LEAF

(Make 6 in Light Green)

With 2mm hook, ch 7, sc in 2nd ch from hook, dc in next 2 ch, sc in next 1 ch, sl st in next ch, 2 sl st in last ch; working around to other side of chain: sl st in next ch, sc in next 1 ch, dc in next 2 ch, sc in last ch, fasten off.

## FINISH

Weave in all ends.

## Top

Lightly steam (WS). Sew neck ties securely to tops of cups, on the inside edge (picot trim). Weave bottom tie through

*(continued next page)*

band: beginning after the 2nd tr, go under 2 sts and over 4 or 5, repeating across, ending before the last 2 tr.

Sew on flowers and leaves: Each cup has 2 tendrils, 1 large leaf, 2 small leaves, 1 double-petal flower, 1(1, 2) medium Apricot flower(s), and 3 White/Yellow flowers (sizes varied). Place as desired along inside edges, starting from the top. Use yarn needle and matching yarn.

## Bottom

Lightly steam underside of skirt and waistband. Weave in waist tie through waistband (follow directions as for Top), starting near one side seam.

Sew on flowers: Each slit has 1 medium Apricot flower, 1 large leaf, and 1 small leaf. Place leaves vertically on top and bottom of flower, or as desired.

*Optional:* Elastic into the waistband. Pin one end of elastic to a side seam, where the waistband and the top of the briefs meet, on the WS. Overlap the seam 2"/5cm. With A and yarn needle, bring needle through a loop just above the

elastic, pull through leaving a 6"/15cm tail, then bring needle through a loop just below the elastic, pull yarn through. Bring the needle through a loop ⅛"/3mm over from the 1st st made, pull through. Bring the needle through a loop just below the elastic, pull through. Rep this process around, encasing the elastic. Tie beg and end of yarn with a square knot. Weave in ends. Now there are two ends of the elastic sticking out between the sts. Put on bottom and pull elastic to desired snugness and safety-pin the ends together. With small needle and thread, sew the two ends of elastic together. Cut off excess and push ends into casing.

**TOP**

**Left Cup**
(Right Cup is same but reversed)

5½(5½)"/14(14)cm

7½(8)"/19(20)cm

3½(4)"/9(10)cm

Dart

Front

6½(7)"/17(18)cm

14½(15½)"/37(39)cm

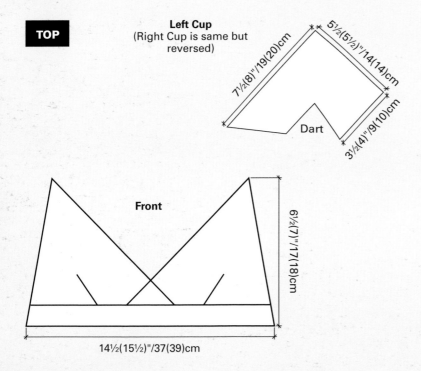

**BRIEFS**

(before waistband and skirt)

Front

2½"/6cm

16(17, 18)"/41(43, 46)cm

Back

15¾(16¼, 16¾)"/40(41, 43)cm

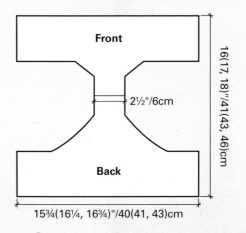

Clint

*Designer:* **Nikol Lohr**

41

Spaghetti Westerns or Marlboro man—
cowboy chic's never been hotter than when
Clint Eastwood sported the look. This felted
"mancho" is a nod to the Man with No Name
and his macho style, which defined a genre.

**LEVEL: INTERMEDIATE**

## Size
Men's One Size Fits All

## Finished Measurements
40–44 x 32–36"/102–118cm x 81–91cm, excluding fringe (finished size will vary somewhat with felting)

## You Will Need
Peruvian Collection Highland Wool (100% wool; 1.75oz/50g = 109yd/99m): (A), 32 skeins, color Tuscany green #7359; (B), 7 skeins, color Bisque #0201—approx 4251yd/3861m of aran-weight yarn, ④

Hook: 4mm/G-6 or size needed to obtain gauge

Cotton waste yarn

Sharp darning needle

Felting needles (optional, for detailing)

## Stitches Used
Chain (ch)

Single crochet (sc)

## Gauge
*Take time to check your gauge.*
12½ sc = 4"/10cm (before felting)
10½ rows = 4"/10cm (before felting)

## Notes
If you haven't done colorwork, don't fret. It's easy! You need to remember only two things.

1. Always start the color on the last loop of the previous color stitch (so you don't get color bleed from the loop of the previous stitch at the top of your first color stitch).

2. Always move yarn to the wrong side before changing colors. Because of the size of this project, you'll often be working with a multitude of bobbins. Pin them just below the colorwork with coilless safety pins, so they don't unravel into a fearsome jumble when you flip the work. Pinning them all down to the wrong side also makes it easier to remember to move your yarn to the wrong side before changing colors. You'll work the whole thing through the top loop only, which creates a somewhat thinner fabric (not too bulky after felting) and speeds progress (taller row height).

## FRONT AND BACK (MAKE 2)

With A, ch 202.

Working into 2nd ch, sc through under-side loop of chain (201 sc). Sc through top loop only, ending with WS row, for 25 rows.

*Next row (RS)*: Begin working from chart (page 44). Chart shows half of the pattern, with the highlighted line marking the center column; simply work the other side in reverse.

As you work, here are a few things to remember:

• Don't forget to start each color change on the last loop of the previous stitch, and always move your yarn to the wrong side before changing colors.

• Don't work the yarn ends in as you go—this would add irregular bulk in felting.

• Snip and knot any floats that are more than a few stitches (they'll pull the fabric too unpredictably in felting), so keep them extra loose so they're long enough—or use bobbins/butterflies as much as is practical.

## Seams

With RS facing, using A and sl st, seam shoulders from edge to just inside S pattern on both sides. This is about right for medium-broad shoulders; for narrower shoulders, seam further in. Weave in yarn ends that terminate on edges of mancho only for about ½"/1cm each, then trim to about 1"/3cm. Instead of weaving in ends on wrong side of colorwork, knot and trim them; cut them off after the fabric has felted and is secure.

## Felt and Finish

Before you get started, take a double strand of the cotton waste yarn and make a running stitch—1 st every 4 sc—about one row up along each bottom edge. This will hold fabric open for the fringe.

Loosely skein one ball of B (wind around swift, niddy-noddy, the back of a chair, your arm, etc., and tie at several points with cotton yarn) and wash it in the machine with hot water on the gentle cycle. This will give you chunky, irregular, felted yarn for the fringe.

At this point, you can choose to go with what you have, or finish it completely with additional details.

If you want to stop here, felt the mancho in the washing machine with hot water and a tablespoon of dish soap until the stitch definition is gone, and it's thick and solid.

Spin on low so it doesn't get creased, then tug horizontally to elongate the pattern a bit. Block edges straight. Allow to dry completely, either flat or folded along seams, flipping occasionally. Snip all yarn ends flush with fabric.

If you want to proceed with the details, lightly felt the mancho to make the detailing easier. You'll be embroidering and needle felting, and it's much easier to work with a denser, more rigid fabric. Machine felt on a short cycle with hot water and a tablespoon of dish soap, checking progress every 5 minutes. Let the fabric felt somewhat, so that it's thicker and less flexible, but still has some stitch definition. Block edges straight and let dry completely.

Take the sharp yarn needle and thread it with a long single strand of A. Using a fairly long (each stitch can cover split stitch, 2 or 3 sc) subdivide the blocks of the bottom border and neck patterns as shown on page 45, then needle-felt to work the stitches firmly into the fabric. (If you aren't familiar with needle felting, just search online for a tutorial).

Machine felt again on a short cycle with hot water, checking every 5 minutes, until the fabric is dense and stitch definition is lost. Spin, block, dry, and trim as above.

When the fabric is completely dry, cut felted yarn into 12"/31cm pieces and fringe the bottom through the cotton-laced holes, one piece of yarn per hole.

# Colorwork Chart

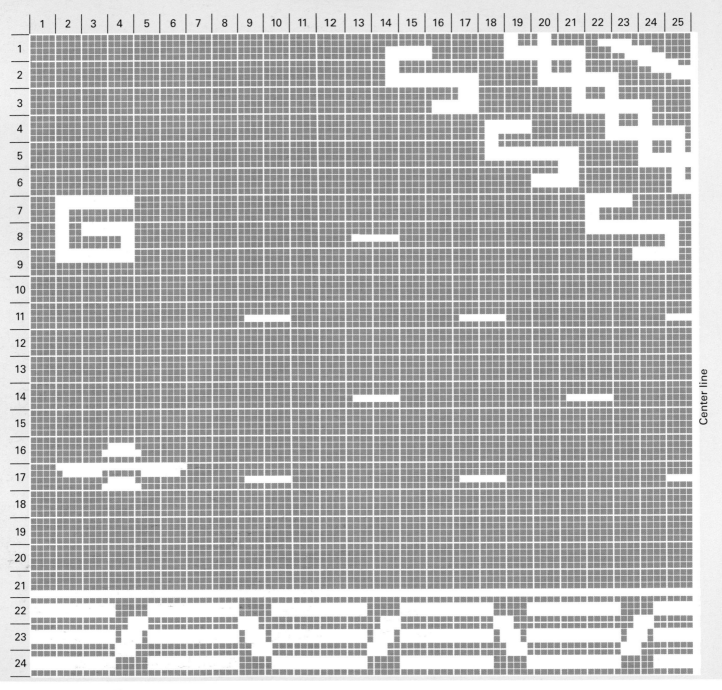

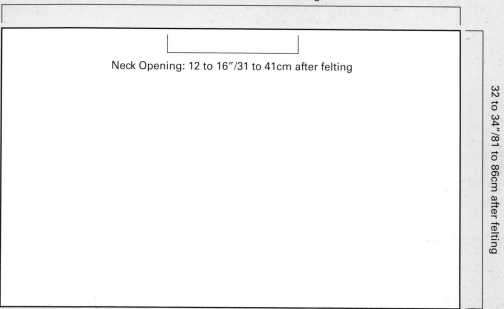

40 to 46"/102 to 117cm after felting

Neck Opening: 12 to 16"/31 to 41cm after felting

32 to 34"/81 to 86cm after felting

**Diagrams for Needle Felting**

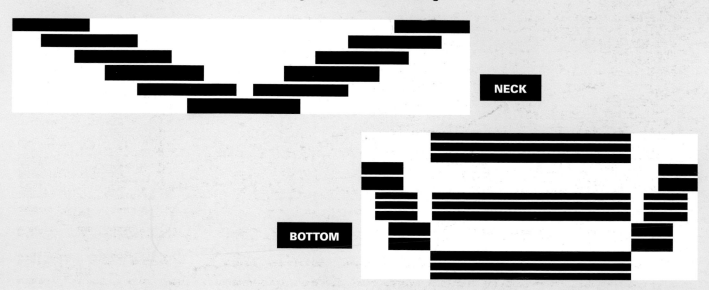

NECK

BOTTOM

*Serena*

Designer: **Vickie Howell**

## Size

S(M, L, XL)

## Finished Measurements

Bust: 31(35, 39, 43)"/
79(89, 99, 109)cm

Length (not including straps):
19(20, 21, 22)"/48(51, 53, 56)cm

## You Will Need

Trendsetter Angel (60% cotton, 31% polyamid, 9% metal; 1.75oz/50g = 85yd/77m): 6(7, 8, 9) skeins, Golden Carnation #400—approx 510(595, 680, 765)yd/462(539, 616, 693)m of heavy worsted-weight yarn, ④

Hooks: 5.5mm/I-9 and 6.5mm/K-10½ or size needed to obtain gauge

Yarn needle

2½ yd/229cm ribbon, approx 1"/3cm wide

Sewing thread

Sewing machine (optional)

## Stitches Used

Chain (ch)

Single crochet (sc)

Double crochet (dc)

Slip stitch (sl st)

## Gauge

*Take time to check your gauge.*

16 sc = 4"/10cm using smaller hook

18 rows = 4"/10cm using smaller hook

**Note:** Front and Back are made identically. Make 2 of each element.

Thanks to Billie Jean King's battle for equality on the court, today's female tennis players can spend less time fighting sexism and more time embracing their strength, determination, and physical power. What could be sexier? Maybe an eye for fashion and a head for business, too (not to mention a killer serve).

## HIP BAND

With smaller hook, ch 17.

Sc in 2nd ch from hook and to end. Turn.

*Next row*: Ch 1, sc in FL of every st to end. Rep last row until piece measures 15½(17½, 19½, 21½)"/ 40(45, 50, 55)cm. Fasten off.

## BODY

With RS facing, pick up a stitch at right top corner of hip band. Ch 1, sc 60(69, 78, 84) sts evenly across top edge of hip band. Turn.

*Next row*: Ch 1, sc to end. Turn.

*Next row*: Ch 7, *skip 2, dc in next st, ch 2; rep from * to end. Turn.

*Next row*: Ch 5, *dc in next dc, ch 2; rep from * to last st, dc. Turn.

Repeat last row until piece measures 15(16, 17, 18)"/38(41, 43, 46)cm.

## SHAPE ARMHOLE

*Next row*: Sl st 9, *dc in next dc, ch 2; rep from * to last 9 sts, sl st to end. Fasten off.

Join yarn at next dc after armhole shaping.

*Next row*: Ch 7, *skip 2, dc in next st, ch 2; rep from * to end, stopping before armhole shaping on opposite side. Turn.

*Next row*: Ch 5, *dc in next dc, ch 2; rep from * to last st, dc. Turn. Repeat last row until piece measures 19(20, 21, 22)"/48(51, 53, 56)cm. Fasten off.

## FINISH

With RS facing, whipstitch front and back pieces together to armhole. Weave in ends. Cut 4 pieces, each 22"/56cm (or desired length) of ribbon for straps.

## STRAPS

Slide piece through one outermost mesh square on one corner, fold piece in half, and sew a straight line down the middle to create a double-layered tie. Rep on rem 3 corners.

*Grace*

Designer: **Vickie Howell**

48

## Size
One Size Fits All

## Finished Measurements
1¾ x 41"/4cm x 104cm (or desired length)

## You Will Need
Lantern Moon/Leigh Radford Silk Gelato (100% silk; 3.5oz/100g= 72yd/66m): 1 ball, color Ice Blue or Butterscotch—approx 72yd/66m of super bulky-weight yarn, (6)

Hook: 9mm/N-13 or size needed to obtain gauge

Yarn needle

Rhinestone or plastic belt buckle

## Stitches Used
Chain (ch)
Half double crochet (hdc)
Slip stitch (sl st)

## Gauge
*Take time to check your gauge.*
10 hdc = 4"/10cm

*Grace Kelly personified elegance. This silk ribbon belt channels her style. Add a vintage rhinestone buckle to turn an otherwise subtle accessory into a classic treasure.*

### BELT
Sl st 4 sts around middle bar on belt buckle. Turn.

*Row 1*: Ch 2 (counts as 1st hdc), hdc in next 3 sts. Turn.

Rep Row 1 until belt measures 41"/104cm or desired length.

Fasten off. Weave in ends.

### VARIATION
For a downtown version of Grace's style, use a modern buckle that rocks a pair of jeans.

50

*Designer:* **Vickie Howell**

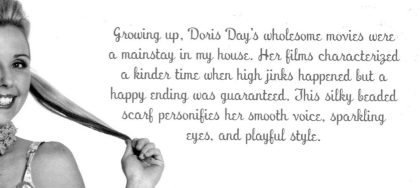

Growing up, Doris Day's wholesome movies were a mainstay in my house. Her films characterized a kinder time when high jinks happened but a happy ending was guaranteed. This silky beaded scarf personifies her smooth voice, sparkling eyes, and playful style.

**Size**
One Size Fits All

**Finished Measurements**
3 x 43"/8 x 109cm

**You Will Need**
Tilli Tomas Rock Star (100% spun silk with glass beads; 3.5oz/100g = 150yd/137m): 1 skein, color Lime Zing—approx 150yd/137m of worsted-weight yarn, (4)

Hook: 4mm/G-6 or size needed to obtain gauge

Yarn needle

**Stitches Used**
Chain (ch)
Single crochet (sc)
Half double crochet (hdc)
Double crochet (dc)
Treble crochet (tr)

**Gauge**
*Take time to check your gauge.*
24 sts = 4"/10cm in pattern st

## SCARF
Ch 24.

***Row 1***: (Sc, ch 3, sc) in 13th ch from hook, *ch 5, skip 5 ch, (sc, ch 3, sc) in next ch; rep from *, ending with ch 5, skip 5, sc in last ch, turn.

***Row 2***: Ch 7, sk 1st sc, skip 5 ch, (sc, ch 3, sc) in next ch-3 loop, *ch 5, (sc, ch 3, sc); rep from *, ending with a ch 5, skip 5, sc in last ch, turn.

Rep Row 2 a total of 68 times; do not fasten off.

## RUFFLE
***Next row***: Ch 4 (counts as 1st tr), 4 tr in same st as ch, ch 5, skip 5 ch, 5 tr in next ch-3 sp, ch 5, skip 5 ch, 5 tr in next ch-3 sp, skip 5 ch, 5 tr in next st. Turn.

***Next row***: Ch 2, hdc to end. Turn.

***Next row***: Ch 3 and dc in same st, 2 dc in next st; rep to end. Fasten off.

Pick up st on corner of opposite end and rep ruffle instructions.

## FINISH
Weave in ends. Block if necessary.

# Shirley

*Designer:* **Stacy Elaine Dacheux**

## Size
Child's S(M, L)

## Finished Measurements
Length: 4(5¾, 7½)"/10(15, 19)cm

## You Will Need
SWTC Karaoke (50% Soysilk, 50% wool; 1.75oz/50g = 109yd/100m): (A), 1(2, 2) skeins, color Black #295—approx 109(218, 218)yd/ 100(200, 200)m of worsted-weight yarn, (**4**)

SWTC Shimmer (50% nylon, 50% polyester; 0.88oz/25g = 150yd/136m): (B), 1 cone, color Madison #405—approx 150yd/136m of fingering-weight yarn, (**1**)

Hook: 5mm/H-8 or size needed to obtain gauge

Yarn needle

Hot pink tulle, ¼ yard

## Stitches Used
Chain (ch)

Single crochet (sc)

## Gauge
*Take time to check your gauge.*

16 sts = 4"/10cm in worsted-weight yarn

16 rows = 4"/10cm in worsted-weight yarn

*Shirley Temple stole the hearts of America with her sweet voice, adorable dimples, and nimble feet, and 65 years later, folks still smile at the mention of her name. These Mary Janes are all about talent and spice, and everything nice.*

## SOLE (MAKE 2)
With A, ch 9(12, 13).

*Next row:* Sc in 2nd ch from hook and across, ch 1, turn [8(11, 12) sc].

Rep last row a total of 14(20, 26) times.

*Next 4 rows:* Sc across, without working turning chains, to slightly round heel. Fasten off.

## TOP (MAKE 2)
With A and B held together, ch 13(15, 17).

*Row 1*: Sc in 2nd ch from hook and across, ch 1, turn [12(14, 16) sc].

*Rows 2–6(8, 12)*: Sc across, ch 1, turn.

*Row 7(9, 13)*: Sc across, fasten off.

## HEEL AND STRAP
With A and B held together, ch 15(20, 21).

*Row 1*: Sc in 2nd ch from hook, sc across, ch 1, turn [14(19, 20) sc].

Work even in sc for 4(7, 9) rows.

*Next row (strap):* Work across in sc, ch 11(14, 17).

Work back in sc across all sts, including ch. Fasten off.

*Note:* For second slipper, be sure to work strap extension chain on opposite side of heel.

## FINISH
Line up the square toe part of the sole with the slipper top. The slipper top is slightly larger than the sole, to allow more toe room. Whipstitch together, easing in fullness. Whipstitch the base of the heel and strap piece to sole, opposite toe. Weave in ends. Cut a piece of tulle 2 x 12"/5 x 30cm and thread it through strap and around back of heel, allowing excess for tying slipper. Trim ends if needed.

Repeat to make other slipper.

# ★ FASHIONISTAS ★

Stephen Chernin/Associated Press

Jennifer Graylock/Associated Press

Stuart Ramson/Associated Press

Designer: **Nikol Lohr**

### Size
Custom

### Finished Measurements
Sleeve width: 10"/25cm or desired width

### You Will Need
Berroco Ultra Silk (20% silk, 40% rayon, 40% nylon; 1.75oz/50g = 98yd/90m): 10–16 skeins (depending on arm length, 10 balls for a shorter woman, 16 for a very tall one), color Cinnabar #6115— approx 980–1568yd/900–1440m of worsted-weight yarn, (4)

Hook: 5.5mm/I-9 or size needed to obtain gauge

Yarn needle

Sewing needle and matching thread (optional)

Fray retardant

### Stitches Used
Chain (ch)
Single crochet (sc)

### Gauge
*Take time to check your gauge.*
16 sc = 4"/10cm
14½ rows = 4"/10cm

### Note
Take two simple measurements to create this shrug.

From the eccentric stylings of Bob Mackie to the layered look of Anna Sui, the figure-flattering kimono sleeve is iconic in shape. The flow of the kimono cut adds an exotic sophistication when applied to a varying range of garments.

### Pattern Notes
Work all foundation rows, including armholes, through underside bumps. Work all other rows through top loop only.

### Yarn Note
The silky yarn can make yarn ends problematic. Apply fray retardant to yarn ends and carefully sew them together with matching sewing thread when you join them. This yarn is somewhat bulky *and* unravels easily, so the fray retardant and drying time is a must. The effort will be worthwhile; make a sample join in your gauge swatch.

### Wool Substitution Note
If you substitute wool for a warmer version, use the actual [A] measurement for sleeves and 80% of [B] for the back. The wool's elasticity changes the nature of the fabric.

### TAKE MEASUREMENTS
With arm outstretched to side, measure from wrist (or between wrist and elbow for three-quarter length sleeves) to point on shoulder where your bra strap rests [A] and from bra strap point to bra strap point between shoulders across throat [B].

### FIRST SLEEVE
Ch 80 (or more if a wider sleeve is desired)

Join with a sl st, being careful not to twist chain.

Work foundation row in sc through the underside bumps of the chain.

Make sure you haven't twisted the rnd before you continue, as both edges will look like the top edge.

Work all subsequent rnds through top loop only.

Spiral around in sc for [A] minus 4"/10cm (or 3"/8cm for ¾-length sleeves), measured flat, finishing out rnd so it ends on the same column as the join. Fabric is stretchy and the weight will make it drape longer than the flat measurement, hence the need to work it shorter than desired. Do not finish off.

## BACK

Armhole round: Sc 15 through top edge, ch 25, skip 25 sts, continue in sc back to chain edge. (Adjust the number of sts chained if needed to create a wider armhole, being sure to skip the same number of sts chained.)

Sc all ch sts through *underside* bumps, then continue as before in sc until back measures 60% of [B]. Back is very stretchy and is best fitted snug.

## SECOND SLEEVE

Rep armhole, being certain to start on the corresponding st from the previous armhole.

Continue until sleeve measures [A] minus 4"/10cm (or 3"/8cm for three-quarter length sleeves), measured flat. Fasten off.

## FINISH

Choose the side you want as the right side and turn garment WS out. Weave in ends with sharp needle, splitting thread to keep secure. Splitting yarn with the sharp needle makes for a more secure weave. If desired, you can carefully tack down all ends with a sewing needle and matching thread.

Machine wash on gentle and tumble dry on low to plump up the fibers and create a cushier garment. The sleeves will be about 1"/3cm narrower, and roughly the same length.

A minus 3 or 4"/8 or 10cm

60% of B

10"/25cm

Vera

Designer: **Robyn Chachula**

58

*Vera Wang incorporates the timeless look of the New York sophisticate into every one of her sought-after wedding dresses. Like Vera's garments, this lacey cashmere sweater captures the essence of the metropolitan woman—both strong and romantic. I implore you, treat yourself to it. You're worth it!*

**LEVEL: INTERMEDIATE**

## Size
S(M, L, XL, 2X, 3X)

## Finished Measurements
Bust: 32(36, 39, 42, 46, 50)"/
81(91, 99, 107, 117, 127)cm
Length: 23(23, 26, 26, 29, 29)"/
58(58, 66, 66, 74, 74)cm

## You Will Need
Karabella Breeze (60% silk,
40% cashmere; 1.75oz/50g =
202yd/184m): 8(9, 11, 12, 13,
14) skeins, color #36—approx
1616(1818, 2222, 2424, 2626, 2828)
yd/1472(1656, 2024, 2208, 2392,
2576)m of DK-weight yarn, ③
Hooks: 3.75mm/F-5 and 4mm/G-6 or
size needed to obtain gauge
Yarn needle
1 button, ⅝"/2mm in diameter
Sewing thread and needle

## Stitches Used
Chain (ch)
Single crochet (sc)
Double crochet (dc)
Treble crochet (tr)
Double treble crochet (dtr)
Slip stitch (sl st)

## Gauge
*Take time to check your gauge.*
2 reps of st patt = 3½ x 4¼"/
9 x 11cm using larger hook

## Pattern Stitch
## (illustrated on page 60)
(multiple of 10 + 8)

**Row 1:** Sc in 12th ch from hook,
*[ch 7, sc in prev ch] 3 times,
ch 4, skip 4 ch, dc in next ch**,
ch 4, skip 4 ch, sc in next ch;
rep from * across, ending at **
in last ch, ch 1, turn.

**Row 2:** *Sc in dc, ch 1, sc in ch-7 sp,
[ch 3, sc in next ch-7 sp] twice,
ch 1; rep from * to end, sc in
turning ch from foundation row,
ch 8, turn.

**Row 3:** Sc in sc, ch 7, sc in prev sc,
ch 4, skip 1 sc, dc in next sc, ch 4,
skip 1 sc, *[ch 7, sc in prev sc]
3 times, ch 4, skip 1 sc, dc in next
sc, ch 4, skip 1 sc; rep from * to
last st, sc in next st, ch 7, sc in
prev sc, ch 3, tr in previous sc,
ch 1, turn.

**Row 4:** Sc in tr, ch 3, sc in ch-7 sp,
ch 1, sc in dc, *ch 1, sc in ch-7 sp,
[ch 3, sc in next ch-7 sp] twice,
ch 1, sc in dc; rep from * to last
ch-7 sp, ch 1, sc in ch-7 sp, ch 3,
sc in turning ch, ch 7, turn.

**Row 5:** Skip 2 sc, sc in next sc, *
[ch 7, sc in prev sc] 3 times, ch 4,
skip 1 sc, dc in next sc**, ch 4,
skip 1 sc, sc in next sc; rep from
* across, ending at ** in last sc,
ch 1, turn.

Rep Rows 2–5 for patt.

*Note:* Top is made in one piece.
*(continued next page)*

## FRONT

With larger hook, ch 98(108, 118, 128, 138, 148). Work in patt st (page 59) until piece measures 13(13, 14½, 14½, 16, 16)"/33(33, 37, 37, 41, 41)cm from beg, ending with Row 4.

## SLEEVES

Ch 118 at end of row, set aside (do not cut yarn).

Join new yarn to top edge of front with sl st to sc at beg of row (opposite end), ch 110, fasten off.

Starting at end of 1st ch (118 ch), work across following Row 1 of patt st. Work in Row 5 across front, and cont on second sleeve (110 ch) in Row 1 again.

Cont as established (next row will be Row 2 on both sleeves and body) until piece measures 20(20, 23, 23, 26, 26)"/51(51, 58, 58, 66, 66)cm, ending with Row 4.

## NECK OPENING

*Next row*: Skip 2 sc, sc in next sc, * [ch 7, sc in prev sc] 3 times, ch 4, skip 1 sc, dc in next sc**, ch 4, skip 1 sc, sc in next sc; rep from * 13 times total (ending at ** in last rep), skip 1 sc, dtr in next sc, ch 1, turn.

*Next row*: Rep Row 2.

*Next row*: Rep Row 3, fasten off.

## OPPOSITE SLEEVE

Skip 4(5, 6, 7, 8, 9) st reps across neck, join new yarn with sl st to sc (above dc) in next patt st.

*Next row*: Ch 5, skip 1 sc, dc in next sc, ch 4, skip next sc, sc in next sc, * [ch 7, sc in prev sc] 3 times, ch 4, skip 1 sc, dc in next sc**, ch 4, skip 1 sc, sc in next sc; rep from * across, ending at ** in last sc, ch 1, turn.

*Next row*: Rep Row 2.

*Next row*: Rep Row 3.

*Next row*: Rep Row 4, fasten off.

## NECK CLOSING

Starting 1 st rep back from neck on last row, join yarn with sl st to sc above middle ch-7 sp.

*Next row*: Ch 61(71, 81, 91, 101, 111), sc in tr in row below, ch 1, cont in Row 4 patt across.

Row 5

Row 4

Row 3

Row 2

Row 1

One Stitch Pattern Repeat

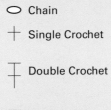

⬭ Chain

✛ Single Crochet

⊤ Double Crochet

⊤ Treble Crochet

## FINISH SLEEVE

Work in Row 5 over sleeves and Row 1 over ch. Cont in patt (next row will be Row 2 across) until piece measures same as for first half of sleeves, ending with Row 4.

## BACK

Skip 10 st reps, join yarn with sl st to middle ch-7 sp of next st. Ch 7.

Beg with Row 5, work in patt until piece measures same as for Front. Fasten off.

## FINISH

Fold sweater in half, sew side seams.

## BAND

With smaller hook, join yarn to bottom of side seam at body opening with sl st. Ch 18.

*Row 1*: Sc in 2nd ch from hook and each ch across, sl st in next 2 ch on Back (1 sl st counts as joining the band to the Back and 1st st counts as the turning ch), turn.

*Row 2*: Skip 2 sl st, sc through the BL of each sc across, ch 1, turn.

*Row 3*: Sc though the BL of each sc across, sl st in next 2 sts on Back.

Rep Rows 2–3 evenly around body opening (to create a gather, skip a ch every 5 ch) until band measures 3"/8cm.

Fasten off, leave long tail for sewing.

Sew band seam closed. Weave in ends.

## EDGE

Sc evenly across sleeve and neck openings with smaller hook.

Sew button to back of neck opening, use open part of front to close.

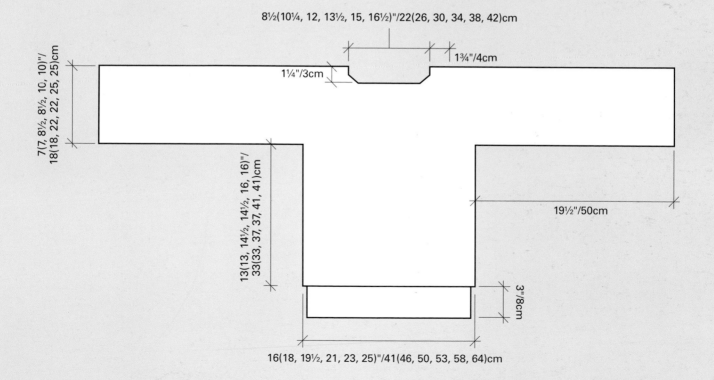

8½(10¼, 12, 13½, 15, 16½)"/22(26, 30, 34, 38, 42)cm

1¾"/4cm

1¼"/3cm

7(7, 8½, 8½, 10, 10)"/18(18, 22, 22, 25, 25)cm

13(13, 14½, 14½, 16, 16)"/33(33, 37, 37, 41, 41)cm

19½"/50cm

3"/8cm

16(18, 19½, 21, 23, 25)"/41(46, 50, 53, 58, 64)cm

# Giselle

Designer: **Jeanette Sherritze**

## Size

XS(S, M, L, XL, 2X, 3X)

## Finished Measurements

Bust: 30(35, 39, 43, 48, 52, 56)"/
76(89, 99, 109, 122, 132, 142)cm
Length: 21(22, 23, 24, 25, 26, 27"/
53(56, 58, 61, 64, 66, 69)cm

## You Will Need

SWTC Bamboo (100% bamboo;
3.5oz/100g = 250yd/228m):
3(4, 5, 6, 7, 8, 9) skeins, color
Butter #129—approx 750(1000,
1250, 1500, 1750, 2000, 2250)
yd/684(912, 1140, 1368, 1596,
1824, 2052)m of DK-weight
yarn, ③

Hook: 2.75mm/C-2 or size needed
to obtain gauge

## Stitches Used

Chain (ch)
Single crochet (sc)
Half double crochet (hdc)
Double crochet (dc)
Double treble crochet (dtr)
Slip stitch (sl st)
Chain Lace (see below)

## Gauge

*Take time to check your gauge.*
20 sc = 4"/10cm
4 lace reps = 7"/18cm

## Pattern Stitch:
## Chain Lace

(Multiple of 10 + 1)

**Row 1**: Ch 2. Dc in 3rd ch from
hook, *skip 4 ch, ch 4, in next ch,
[sc, ch 7] 3 times, sc in same ch,
skip 4 ch, ch 4, dc in next ch; rep
from * to last st, dc.

**Row 2 (RS)**: Turn. Ch 1, *sc in dc,
ch 1, [sc in ch-7 loop, ch 3] 2
times, sc in ch-7 loop, ch 1;
rep from * across, ending
with sc in dc, skip t-ch.

**Row 3**: Turn. Ch 1. In sc work
[ch 7, sc] 2 times, *skip (ch-
1, sc, ch-3), ch 4, dc in sc,
skip (ch-3, sc, ch-1), ch 4, in
sc work [sc, ch 7] 3 times,
sc in same sc; rep from *,
ending with (sc, ch 7, sc,
ch 4, dtr) in sc, skip t-ch.

**Row 4**: Turn. Ch 1. Sc in ch-7
loop, ch 3, sc in ch-7 loop,
*ch 1, sc in dc, ch 1, [sc in
ch-7 loop, ch 3] 2 times, sc
in ch-7 loop; rep from *
across, ending with ch 3,
sc in ch-7 loop.

**Row 5**: Turn. Ch 2. *Dc in sc,
skip (ch 3, sc, ch 4), in sc
work [sc, ch 7] 3 times, sc in
same sc, skip (ch 1, sc, ch 3);
rep from * across, ending with
dc in sc, skip t-ch.

Rep Rows 2–5 for pattern, ending
with Row 2 or 4.

*(continued next page)*

*A lacey corset made from
bamboo yarn celebrates
Brazilian model Gisele
Bündchen's best-known
attributes: femininity and
environmental awareness.*

## BODY

*Note:* Connect each strip to the previous strip(s) as it is completed, do not join last strip to first strip (leave flat).

Crochet 7(8, 9, 10, 11, 12, 13) strips of Chain Lace pattern (page 63), beginning each with ch 21 and cont in pattern until piece measures 9½"/24cm, ending after Row 2 or 4.

Connect strips along long edges as follows: On working strip, starting from upper left corner, ch 4, sl st to top right corner of previous strip (on top of dc); sc in middle of same dc one st below on same long edge of strip; turn, 3 sc across ch to 1st strip. Sl st into edge st on strip; sc in next row on same edge as sl st just made, *ch 4, sl st into edge st on opposite strip, sc, turn, 3 sc across ch. Sl st into edge st on next row of adjacent strip. Sc in next row on same strip. Turn. [Long dc into sc of row below (insert hook in row below, make dc, bringing st up to level of current row) in 3-st bridge] 2 times, sc in next st on ch. Sl st in next row on strip, sc in next row of same strip; rep from * to 1 row before end.

*Last row (RS):* In ch, [long hdc in row below] 2 times; sc in next st on ch. Sl st to working strip in bottom edge corner st, ch 1, fasten off.

## BOTTOM BORDER

*Row 1*: With RS facing, join yarn. Ch 1, sc 161(181, 201, 221, 241, 261, 281) across bottom of strips.

*Row 2*: Ch 1, sc in 1st sc and in each sc across of row just made.

*Row 3*: Work Row 1 of Chain Lace pattern.

*Row 4*: Work Row 2 of Chain Lace pattern.

Fasten off.

## UPPER BODICE

With RS facing, join yarn. Ch 1, sc 161 (181, 201, 221, 241, 261, 281) across top of strips. Place markers 40(45, 50, 55, 60, 65, 70) from each end (for sides).

Next row: Ch 1, sc across.

Work in Chain Lace pattern for 2(2½, 3, 3½, 4, 4½, 5)"/5(6, 8, 9, 10, 11, 13)cm.

## DIVIDE FOR ARMHOLES

Continue in Chain Lace pattern, working sl sts over 5(5, 10, 10, 10, 10, 10) sts each side of each side marker [1(1, 2, 2, 2, 2, 2) rep(s) of pattern], maintaining pattern as established on other sts, adjusting as needed.

## LEFT FRONT

Cont in Chain Lace pattern on left front only, dec 1 st at each edge (front and armhole) every row until 11 sts (1 st pattern) rem. Work even in pattern until armhole measures 7(7½, 8, 8½, 9, 9½, 10)"/18(19, 21, 22, 23, 24, 25)cm, ending with Row 2 or 4. Fasten off.

## RIGHT FRONT

Join yarn and work as for Left Front, cont in Chain Lace pattern as established.

## BACK

Join yarn at back at armhole edge. Cont in Chain Lace pattern as established, dec 1 st each side every row 10(10, 15, 15, 20, 20, 20) times; 51(61, 61, 71, 71, 81, 91) sts. Work even until piece measures 2"/5cm less than front.

*Next row*: Work across 1 rep of pattern, sl st across to last rep of pattern, work last rep.

Working each side separately, cont in pattern on straps until piece measures same as front. Fasten off.

## FINISH

Join shoulder seams with sc. Work 2 rnds of sc around armholes. Work 1 row of sc around front edges and neck, beginning and ending at lower edges of front.

*Next row*: *Ch 3, sl st in 1st ch from hook, ch 2, skip 4 sc, 2 sc; rep from * to start of front shaping, sc to same point on opposite side, rep from * to end, fasten off.

Weave in ends.

## CORD

Ch 200(210, 220, 230, 240, 250, 260). Sc in 2nd st from hook and across. Fasten off.

Thread cord through loops on fronts and tie ends at top.

Yohji

*Designer:* **Allison Whitlock**

## Size
S(M/L): 6–8(10–12)

## Finished Measurements
Length: 36"/91cm

Shoulder width: 25"/64cm

Bust: 34–36"/86–91cm

## You Will Need
Karabella Labirinth (57% merino, 12% superkid mohair, 17% polyamid, 14% polyacrylic; 1.75oz/50g = 81yd/74m): 12(12) skeins, color #31308—approx 972(972)yd/888(888)m of heavy worsted-weight yarn, ④

Hook: 5.5mm/I-9 or size needed to obtain gauge

5yd/5m of chocolate brown leather lacing

Scrap yarn for marking

Yarn needle

## Stitches Used
Chain (ch)

Double crochet (dc)

## Gauge
*Take time to check your gauge.*

10 dc = 4"/10cm

8 rows = 4"/10cm

---

*Asymmetrical design made a huge splash in Japan several years ago and has since become popular in the States and the UK. This high-fashion wrap-sweater, inspired by the ingenious Yohji Yamamoto, is simply designed and brilliantly assembled.*

Starting at the bottom edge, ch 43(46).

**Row 1**: Dc in 4th ch from hook, dc in each ch across, turn, [40(43) dc].

**Row 2**: Ch 3, dc in each dc across, turn.

Rep Row 2 until work measures 66"/168cm

Fasten off.

At this point weave in ends, or knot and leave them for a more deconstructed look.

### FINISH
Piecing together is the most complicated part of this project. To make things easier, use scrap yarn to mark out the beginning and end points of each seam. The number of strands you use will indicate the marker number and will correspond to a matching point on the alternate side of the garment.

**Step 1**: Lay work out flat with shortest side closest to you. With scrap yarn, mark the following points around the perimeter of your crocheted rectangle. Refer to figure 1 (next page).

### Left side
L1: Bottom left corner (mark with 1 strand)

L2: 7½"/19cm from bottom (mark with 2 strands)

L3: 15½"/39cm from bottom (mark with 3 strands)

L4: 25½"/65cm from bottom (mark with 4 stands)

L5: 35"/89cm from bottom (mark with 5 strands)

L6: 45"/114cm from bottom (mark with 5 strands)

### Right side
R1: 29"/74cm from bottom (mark with 1 strand)

R2: 36½"/93cm from bottom (mark with 2 strands)

R3: 50"/127cm from bottom (mark with 3 strands)

R4: 60"/152cm from bottom (mark with 4 strands)

### Top (from left)
T6: Top left corner (mark with 6 strands)

T5: 10"/25cm from left (mark with 5 strands)

**Step 2**: With WS facing, bring the left side to the right and pin together markers L1 and R1, L2 and R2, then tack a seam with project yarn between these two points. Remove markers.

**Step 3**: Flip garment over and with WS facing, pin together markers L3 and R3, L4 and R4, then tack a seam between these two points. Remove markers.

**Step 4**: Flip garment to face the front and with WS facing, pin together markers L5 and T5, L6 and T6. Tack a seam between these two points. Remove markers. Your sweater should look like figure 2.

**Step 5**: With leather lacing, sc from marker 1 to 6, keeping seams together where tacked and open at sleeves.

**Step 6**: Remove tacking. With leather lacing create an uneven 10"/25cm fringe and attach at the longest point of your garment with a crochet hook.

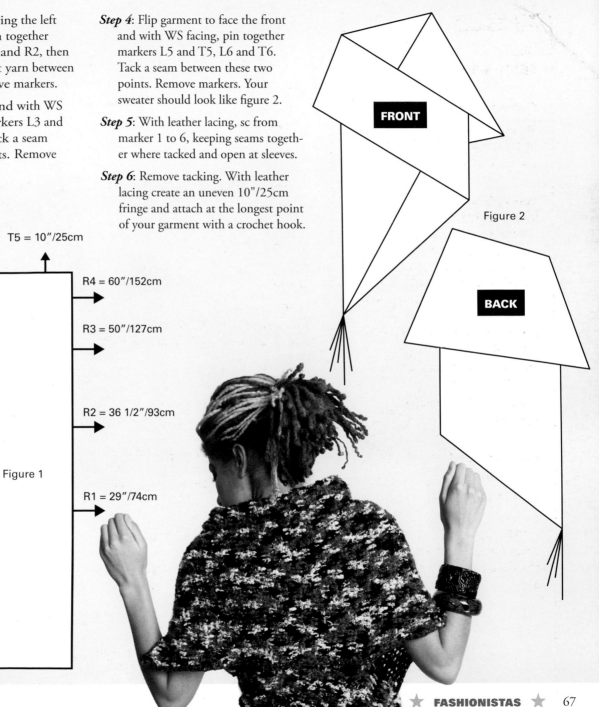

Figure 2

FRONT

BACK

T6 = 0"/0cm

T5 = 10"/25cm

R4 = 60"/152cm

R3 = 50"/127cm

L6 = 45"/114cm

R2 = 36 1/2"/93cm

L5 = 35"/89cm

Figure 1

R1 = 29"/74cm

L4 = 25 1/2"/65cm

L3 = 15 1/2"/39cm

L2 = 7 1/2"/19cm

L1 = 0"/0cm

# Betsey

Designer: **Stephanie Ryan**

Playful style that's part pretty, part punk is the signature of designer Betsey Johnson. Crochet a tribute to the woman who makes whimsy workable and edgy ageless. This one goes out to all those who march to the beat of a different drum.

**LEVEL: BEGINNER**

## Size
Girl's 4(6, 8)

## Finished Measurements
Chest: 23(25, 27)"/58(64, 69)cm
Length (excluding straps): Approx 15(21, 24)"/38(53, 61)cm

## You Will Need
Berroco Cotton Twist (70% mercerized cotton, 30% rayon; 1.75oz/50g = 85yd/77m): (A), 9(10, 12) skeins, color Pitch Black #8390; (B), 1 skein, color Radish #8351; (C), 1 skein, color Sassafras #8349—approx 935(1020, 1190) yd/847(924, 1078)m of worsted-weight yarn, (4)

Hooks: 4mm/G-6 and 5mm/H-8 standard hooks, 6mm/J-10 Tunisian hook or size needed to obtain gauge

4(5, 6) shank buttons, hot pink, ⁷/₁₆"/1cm diameter

24(26, 28)"/61(66, 71)cm elastic, black, ½"/1cm wide
7¾(8¾, 9)yd/7(8, 8)m tulle, hot pink
Yarn needle
Sewing needle and black thread
8 black beads

## Stitches Used
Chain (ch)
Single crochet (sc)
Half double crochet (hdc)
Double crochet (dc)
Tunisian Simple Stitch (tss) (*see below*)
Reverse single crochet (rev sc)
Slip stitch (sl st)

## Gauge
*Take time to check your gauge.*
18 sc = 4"/10cm using 5mm hook
14 tss = 4"/10cm using 6mm Tunisian hook
12 rows = 4"/10 cm using 6mm Tunisian hook

## Stitch Pattern:
### Tunisian Simple Stitch (tss)
Worked through the front vertical bar of the prior row, with Tunisian hook.

The forward pass begins with a single loop on the hook from the prior row. Skip the first vertical bar, insert hook into next vertical bar, yarn over, and pull it through, leaving the stitch on the hook. Rep to end of row, leaving all stitches on the hook. Now you're ready for the reverse pass.

Once the forward pass is complete and all loops are on the hook, yarn over and draw through 1 loop only.

After this 1st st, *yarn over, draw through 2 loops. Rep from * until only 1 st rem on the hook. Don't turn.

(*continued next page*)

## BODICE

With A and 5mm crochet hook, ch 105 (114, 123).

**Row 1**: Sc in 2nd ch from hook and in each ch across 104(113, 122) sc.

**Row 2**: Ch 1, turn. Working through the BLs only, sc across.

**Row 3**: Rep Row 2 a total of 20(26, 31) times. Do not fasten off.

## SKIRT

With A and Tunisian hook, begin at last st of bodice with RS facing.

**Row 1 (Forward pass)**: *Pull up 2 loops in 1st sc (pull up 1 loop through the FL only, then 1 loop through both loops of the same st to inc), pull up 1 loop in each of next 2 sc; rep from * across, end 1 loop in each of next 2 sc [138(150, 162) loops). Reverse pass: Standard tss.

**Row 2**: Tss in each st across.

**Row 3**: Rep Row 2, 35(49, 56) times more.

Change to B for forward pass and C for reverse pass on rows indicated: [Size 4: Rows 7, 18, 35; Size 6: Rows 11, 28, 49; Size 8: Rows 14, 32, 56].

**Finishing row**: Sl st in each vertical bar across. Rev sc back across each sl st just made.

Fasten off, leaving approx 20"/51cm long tail for seaming.

## BUTTONHOLE ROW

With A and 5mm crochet hook, RS facing, join with sl st in base ch row of left bodice edge.

*Row 1*: Ch 1, sc in same st and in each row end across [22(28, 34) sc].

*Row 2*: Turn, sl st in 1st st, ch 2, skip 2 sc, *sl st in next 4 sc, ch 2, skip 2 sc; rep from * to last st, sl st in last sc [4(5, 6) ch-2 sp].

## BODICE EDGE

With A and 5mm crochet hook, RS facing, join with sl st to last row worked on right bodice edge, near skirt.

*Row 1*: Ch 1, sc in same st and in each st across side and top of bodice, (sc, ch 1, sc) in corner st.

*Row 2*: Do not turn, work 1 rev sc in each sc made.

## STRAPS

Lay dress folded as it would be worn. Mark sts that are 3(3 1/2, 4)"/8(9, 10)cm from center point on front and back of bodice. With C and 5mm hook, using a double strand of yarn, ch 15(17, 19). Fasten off, leaving a 10"/25cm tail. Sew strap to one of the marked sts with long tail at end for beads, rep for other 3 straps.

## FLOWER (MAKE 6)

With B and 4mm crochet hook, ch 2.

*Rnd 1*: Sc in 2nd ch from hook, *ch 3, dc in same st, sl st into same st; rep from * 4 times more. Fasten off. Pull tails tightly to close flower.

## LEAF (MAKE 4)

With C and 4mm crochet hook, ch 6.

*Row 1*: Sl st into 2nd ch from hook, sc, hdc, 3 dc. Working in free loops on opposite side of ch, hdc, sc, sl st to end. Fasten off.

## FINISH

Seam skirt, weave in ends. Block dress, with particular attention to skirt, as Tunisian crochet tends to curl. Allow to dry completely.

## Straps

Knot both tails together 7"/18cm from last ch made on each strap. Thread 1 bead onto each tail and knot to secure, leaving one beaded tail approx ½"/1cm longer than the other. Trim tails. With yarn needle and tails on flowers and leaves, attach 3 flowers and 2 leaves to each front strap. With sewing needle and thread, attach 1 bead to each flower motif center.

## Bodice

Sew buttons opposite buttonholes.

## Tulle Underskirt

Fold tulle in half lengthwise. Fold in thirds so there are 6 layers and it measures 92(100, 108)"/234(254, 274)cm across top edge. With sewing needle and thread, weave in and out loosely about ½"/1cm from top edge. Pull ends gently to gather tulle until top edge measures 23(25, 27)"/58(64, 69)cm, secure with knots. Sew elastic to gathered edge of tulle, taking care not to stretch elastic. Seam side of underskirt. Trim seams evenly. Sew elastic band to inside of dress at the base of the last bodice row. Trim tulle so that it peeks out from under skirt 4"/10cm.

*Harlow*

*Designer:* **Libby Bailey**

These days, celebrity babies leave the womb ready to make a fashion statement. With the world's eyes upon them, infants like Suri, Harlow, Emme, and Max all wear clothes to die for while still in diapers! Our silky baby sacque adds glam to nap time.

### Size
0–6 months

### Finished Measurements
Chest: Approx 20"/51cm

### You Will Need
Berroco Softwist (59% rayon, 41% wool; 1.75oz/50g = 100yd/91m): (A), 1 skein, color Delphinium #9419—approx 100yd/91m of worsted-weight yarn,

SWTC Vickie Howell Collection Love (70% bamboo, 30% silk; 1.75oz/50g = 99yd/90m): (B), 1 skein, Lloyd & Diane #243— approx 99yd/90m of worsted-weight yarn, ❹

Hooks: 3.75mm/F-5 and 5mm/H-8 or size needed to obtain gauge

13 x 36"/33cm x 91cm piece of fabric

Fusible web or sewing needle and thread

Yarn needle

Large-eye embroidery needle

4 small buttons (size to match crocheted button loops, approx ½"/1cm in diameter)

Embroidery thread to match B

### Stitches Used
Chain (ch)

Single crochet (sc)

Double crochet (dc)

Slip stitch (sl st)

### Gauge
*Take time to check your gauge.*
16 dc = 4"/10cm using larger hook

8 rows = 4"/10cm using larger hook

### FRONT
With larger hook and A, loosely ch 42 sts.

*Row 1*: In 2nd chain from hook, sc, then sc in each chain across, ch 1, turn (40 sc).

*Row 2*: Sc across, ch 2, turn.

*Rows 3–6*: Dc in each sc across, ch 2, turn (omit ch 2 on Row 6).

*(continued next page)*

## SHAPE ARMHOLE

**Row 7**: Sl st the 1st 7 sts, ch 2, dc to last 7 sts, turn (do not work last 7 sts).

**Row 8**: Dc across last dc row, ch 2, turn. Rep Row 8 until piece measures 2"/5cm above underarm.

## STRAPS

**Next row**: Dc in 1st 7 sts; ch 2, turn.

Dc these 7 sts for 5 more rows, cut yarn, pull yarn through last st to fasten off.

Join yarn at the other side of piece and work the 1st 7 sts same as for prev strap.

## BACK

Work same as for Front, working straps 1 row longer than on Front. Fasten off.

## FINISH

With WS together, slip st or sc the Front to the Back at the sides.

With smaller hook and B, sc around armholes, straps (at the top edge of each back strap, make a button loop at each corner by ch 4, then sc in next st), neck, and back.

Join with a sl st, cut yarn, and fasten off.

Join B to the bottom edge of piece, sc around. Join with sl st, cut yarn, fasten off.

## FABRIC SACQUE

Fold all edges of fabric under ¼"/6mm, then ¼"/6mm again. Finish these edges with fusible web or needle and thread.

Fold fabric in half lengthwise so it measures 12 x 17"/30 x 43cm.

With RS together, sew side seams.

Thread all 6 strands of embroidery thread through a large-eye embroidery needle, then blanket-stitch around the entire top edge of the sacque. Sts should be about ¼"/6mm apart (you will be crocheting through these blanket st loops).

## EDGING

With WS together, B, and smaller hook, sc around top edge of sacque, working through blanket stitching. Join with sl st; ch 1. Work 1 more rnd in sc.

Join with sl st, but *do not* tie off yarn; retain the working loop.

Turn sacque so RS are together; turn crocheted top so WS are together.

Slip top into sacque, straps first, then match the bottom edge of the crocheted top to the top edge of the fabric sacque.

Matching side seams of both pieces, pin the top piece to the sacque.

Pick up the working loop from the sacque crocheted edge, then sc the two pieces together. Be sure to put the hook through both loops of each st as you join the two pieces. Turn to RS.

Sew 2 buttons to each front strap, placed to correspond with the button loops on the back straps.

Weave in ends.

Designer: **Jeanette Sherritze**

75

## Size
Small

## Finished Measurements
Bust: 30"/76cm

Length: 25"/64cm

## You Will Need
SWTC Shimmer (50% nylon, 50% polyester; 0.88oz/25g = 150yd/136m): 6 cones, color Go Gold #405—approx 900yd/816m of fingering-weight yarn,

Hook: 2.75mm/C-2 or size needed to obtain gauge

## Stitches Used
Chain (ch)

Single crochet (sc)

Double crochet (dc)

Treble crochet (tr)

Slip stitch (sl st)

Beginning Shell Stitch *(see below)*

Shell Stitch *(see below)*

## Gauge
*Take time to check your gauge.*

1 medallion = 5"/13cm square

## Pattern Stitches:
**Beginning Shell Stitch (Beg Shell St)**

Ch 3 (counts as 1st dc), (dc, ch 3, 2 dc) in same st

**Shell Stitch (Shell St)**

(2 dc, ch 3, 2 dc) in same st

---

*Secluded islands, penthouse pools, and private yachts are the playgrounds of daddy's privileged little princess, and "made up with martini" is the sun-bathing requirement for celebutantes, starlets, and trophy wives. With this glitzy, golden cover-up, you'll have a poolside presence that even Paris Hilton would envy!*

## MEDALLIONS (MAKE 6)

**Rnd 1**: Ch 8, sl st into 1st st to join for ring.

**Rnd 2**: Ch 3 (counts as 1st dc), 31 dc in ring; sl st in top of 1st dc to join rnd (32 dc).

**Rnd 3**: In sl st, work Beg Shell St, *ch 7, skip 3 dc, Shell St in top of next dc, rep from * 6 times more, forming 8 equally spaced Shell Sts; end ch 7, sl st in top of 1st dc to join rnd.

**Rnd 4**: Sl st to middle of ch-3 sp, work Beg Shell St in ch-3 sp, * ch 7, skip ch-7 sp; Shell St in next ch-3 sp, rep from * 6 times more; end ch 7, sl st in top of 1st dc to join rnd.

**Round 5**: Sl st to middle of ch-3 sp, work Beg Shell St in ch-3 sp, *ch 4, sc over both ch-7 sps from prev 2 rnds, ch 4; Shell St in next ch-3 sp, rep from * 6 times more; end ch 4, sc over both ch-7 sps from prev 2 rnds, ch 4, sl st in top of 1st dc of Beg Shell St to join rnd.

**Rnd 6**: Sl st to middle of ch-3 sp, work Beg Shell St in ch-3 sp, *ch 16, sl st in 12th ch from hook (forming ring); ch 3, sl st to top of last dc of prev Shell St. Turn so you can crochet into the ring, dc 6 times in ring. Sl st in sc from prev rnd (anchoring half circle to medallion, dc 8 times more in ring, forming a half circle, which will be completed later). Shell St in next ch-3 sp; rep from *rep 6 times more. Complete Rnd 6 as follows:

**On 1st Medallion**: Ch 16, sl st in 11th ch from hook to form ring, ch 3, sl st in top of last dc of Shell St, turn, dc 6 times in ring, sl st in sc from prev rnd, dc 8 times more in ring to complete. Sl st into top of 1st dc of 1st Shell St of rnd.

**On all medallions after 1st**: Join to prev finished medallion as follows: Sl st into top of last dc on outer edge of 8th circle on prev medallion, sl st 7 times more in tops of dcs of 8th ring of finished medallion, sl st to working medallion in sc of prev row; sl st 8 times more in ring of finished medallion, completing half circle; sl st into top of 1st dc of working medallion.

**Rnd 7**: On 1st medallion, to begin: Sl st to ch-3 sp, ch 1, dc in ch-3 sp, ch 6, sl st in 4th ch from hook

(forming picot), dc in same ch-3 sp, ch 1, proceed to *. On all medallions after 1st, to begin: Sl st to ch-3 sp, ch 1, dc in ch-3 sp, sc in corresponding picot of prev medallion, dc in same ch-3 sp, ch 1, proceed to *.

*Sl st to 1st ch of ch 16 from prev rnd, 16 dc into ring, sl st to top of 1st dc of Shell St from prev rnd; ch 1, dc in ch-3 sp, ch 6, sl st into 4th ch from hook, dc into same ch-3 sp, ch 1; rep from * to last circle, complete Rnd 7 as follows:

**On 1st medallion, to end**: Sl st to 1st ch of ch 16 from prev rnd, 16 dc into ring, sl st to ch 1.

**On all medallions after 1st, to end**: Sl st to top of dc on conjoined ring. Sl st again. Fasten off.

## MEDALLION BORDER

Join yarn with a sl st in top of dc on middle circle of strip edge (short side).

Ch 9, *sl st in picot point, ch 4, dc in 5th dc of circle, ch 7, sl st in 2nd chain from hook, ch 5, tr in 11th dc on circle (on long side), ch 4, sl st in picot point, ch 9, sl st in 8th dc of circle, ch 9, sl st in picot point, ch 5, tr in 5th dc on circle, ch 10, rep from *rep across medallion strip; following last tr of row, ch 7, sl st in 2nd ch from hook, ch 5, dc in 11th dc on circle (on short side), ch 4, sl st in picot point, ch 9, sl st in 8th dc on ring, ch 4, sl st in picot point, ch 5 in 5th dc on ring, ch 7, sl st in 2nd ch from hook, *ch 5, tr in 11th dc on circle (on long side), ch 4, sl st in picot point, ch 9, sl st in 8th dc of circle, ch 9, sl st in picot

*(continued next page)*

point, ch 5, tr in 5th dc on circle, ch 10; rep from * across medallion strip; following last tr of row, ch 7, sl st in 2nd ch from hook, ch 5, dc in top of 11th dc on circle (on short side), ch 9, sl st in 1st ch. Fasten off.

## ROW OF CIRCLES FOR DRAWSTRING

Join yarn in outer corner of border. Dc in every st across row. Turn. Ch 4, sl st into 1st ch from hook, ch 6, sl st in 1st ch to form ring, 4 hdc in ring, sl st to 5th dc from outer edge on prev row, 5 hdc in ring, ch 2, sl st into 1st ch (half of 1st circle completed plus ch-2 sp between circles). *Ch 6, sl st in 5th chain from hook to form ring, 4 hdc in ring, skip 4 dc, sl st in next dc, 5 hdc in ring; ch 2, sl st in 1st ch; rep from * to end, tr to join to edge. Turn. *9 hdc in ring (completes top of 1st circle), sl st in 1st hdc of prev row on circle, sc over ch-2 sp; rep from * to end, sl st in top of 1st dc of circle. Turn.

Ch 4, sl st in ch next to hook, ch 3, *sl st in top of 5th dc on ring, ch 5; rep from * across, end with ch 4, sl st into ch next to hook; tr to top of tr of prev row.

*Next row*: Ch 3 (counts as 1st dc), dc in every st across row.

## FOUNDATION ROW FOR TOP

*Row 1*: With RS facing, work Beg Shell St in top of 1st dc, *ch 5, skip 6 dc, dc in top of next dc, ch 5, skip 6 dc, Shell St in top of next dc; rep from * across row. Turn.

*Row 2*: Begin this row (and all other rows) by sl st to center of ch-3 sp in Shell on RS edge, work Beg Shell St, *ch 5, dc in top of next dc, ch 5, Shell St in next ch-3 sp of Shell st from prev row; rep from * to end. Turn.

*Row 3*: Rep Row 1.

## FRONT
### Shape Left Front

*Note:* Shaping rows are not worked across entire width of garment.

*Row 4*: Beginning at front edge, work Beg Shell St, ch 3, *dc in top of dc, ch 5, Shell St in ch-3 sp of Shell St from prev row, ch 5; rep from * 2 times more, end row with dc in top of next dc, ch 4, Shell St in next ch-3 sp. Turn.

*Row 5*: Beg at armhole edge, work Beg Shell St in ch-3 sp, ch 3, *dc in top of next dc, ch 5, Shell St in ch-3 sp, ch 5; rep from * 2 times more, dc in top of next dc, ch 3, Shell St in last ch-3 sp. Turn.

*Row 6*: Work Beg Shell St, ch 2, *dc in top of next dc, ch 5, Shell St in next ch-3 sp, ch 5; rep from * 2 times more, dc in top of next dc, ch 1, Shell St in next ch-3 sp.

*Row 7*: Work Beg Shell St in ch-3 sp, *dc in top of next dc, ch 5, Shell St in next ch-3 sp, ch 5; rep from * 2 times more, dc in top of next dc, ch 2, Shell St in last ch-3 sp. Turn.

*Row 8*: Work Beg Shell St in ch-3 sp, ch 1, *dc in top of next dc, ch 5, Shell St in next ch-3 sp, ch 5; rep from * 2 times more, ch 5, Shell St in next ch-3 sp, ch 4, dc in top of next dc, Shell St in last ch-3 sp. Turn.

**Row 9**: Work Beg Shell St in ch-3 sp, ch 3, *Shell St in next ch-3 sp, ch 5, dc in top of next dc, ch 5; rep from * 1 time more, Shell St in next ch-3 sp, ch 4, dc in top of next dc, ch 1, Shell St in last ch-3 sp. Turn.

**Row 10**: Work Beg Shell St in ch-3 sp, dc in top of next dc, ch 4, *Shell St in next ch-3 sp, ch 5, dc in top of next dc, ch 5; rep from * 1 time more, Shell St in next ch-3 sp, ch 2, Shell St in last ch-3 sp. Turn.

**Row 11**: Work Beg Shell St in ch-3 sp, ch 1, Shell St in next ch-3 sp, ch 4, dc in top of next dc, ch 5, Shell St in next ch-3 sp, ch 5, dc in top of next dc, ch 5, Shell St in next ch-3 sp, ch 2, dc in top of next dc, Shell St in last ch-3 sp. Turn.

**Row 12**: Work Beg Shell St in ch-3 sp, ch 1, *Shell St in next ch-3 sp, ch 4, dc in top of next dc, ch 4; rep from * 1 time more, Shell St in ch-3 sp, Shell St in last ch-3 sp. Turn.

**Row 13**: Work Beg Shell St in ch-3 sp, sc in ch 2 of ch-3 sp, ch 4, dc in top of next dc, ch 4, Shell St in next ch-3 sp, ch 4, dc in top of next dc, ch 4, Shell St in next ch-3 sp, Shell St in last ch-3 sp. Turn.

**Row 14**: Work Beg Shell St in ch-3 sp, sc in ch 2 of ch-3 sp, ch 4, dc in top of next dc, ch 4, Shell St in next ch-3 sp, ch 4, dc in top of next dc, ch 4, Shell St in last ch-3 sp. Turn.

**Row 15**: Work Beg Shell St in ch-3 sp, ch 3, dc in top of next dc, ch 3, Shell St

in next ch-3 sp, ch 3, dc in top of next dc, ch 3 Shell St in last ch-3 sp. Turn.

**Rows 16–23**: Rep Row 15.

**Row 24 (shape neck)**: Work Beg Shell St in ch-3 sp, ch 3, dc in top of next dc, ch 3, Shell St in next ch-3 sp, ch 3, sc in top of next dc, sl st in next st. Fasten off.

## Shape Right Front

Join yarn at right front edge with RS facing.

**Row 4**: Beg at front edge, work Beg Shell St in ch-3 sp, ch 3, *dc in top of next dc, ch 5, Shell St in next ch-3 sp, ch 5; rep from * 2 times more, dc in top of next dc, ch 3, Shell St in next ch-3 sp. Turn.

**Row 5**: Beg at armhole edge, work Beg Shell St in ch-3 sp, ch 2, *dc in top of next dc, ch 5, Shell St in next ch-3 sp, ch 5; rep from * 2 times more, dc in top of next dc, ch 3, Shell St in next ch-3 sp. Turn.

**Row 6**: Work Beg Shell St in ch-3 sp, ch 2, * dc in top of next dc, ch 5, Shell St in next ch-3 sp, ch 5; rep from * 2 times more, dc in top of next dc, ch 1, Shell St in next ch-3 sp. Turn.

**Row 7**: Work Beg Shell St in ch-3 sp, *dc in top of next dc, ch 5, Shell St in next ch-3 sp, ch 5; rep from * 2 times more, dc in top of next dc, ch 2, Shell St in last ch-3 sp. Turn.

**Row 8**: Work Beg Shell St in ch-3 sp, ch 1, dc in top of next dc, ch 4, *Shell St in next ch-3 sp, ch 5, dc in top of next dc, ch 5; rep from *

1 time more, Shell St in next ch-3 sp, ch 4, Shell St in last ch-3 sp. Turn.

**Row 9**: Work Beg Shell St in ch-3 sp, ch 3, Shell St in next ch-3 sp, *ch 5, dc in top of next dc, ch 5, Shell St in next ch-3 sp; rep from * 1 time more, Shell St in next ch-3 sp, ch 4, dc in top of next dc, Shell St in last ch-3 sp. Turn.

**Row 10**: Work Beg Shell St in ch-3 sp, dc in top of next dc, ch 3, Shell St in next ch-3 sp, ch 5, dc in top of next dc, ch 5, Shell St in next ch-3 sp, ch 5, dc in top of next dc, ch 4, Shell St in next ch-3 sp, ch 2, Shell St in last ch-3 sp. Turn.

**Row 11**: Work Beg Shell St in ch-3 sp, ch 1, Shell St in next ch-3 sp, *ch 4, dc in top of next dc, ch 4, Shell St in next ch-3 sp; rep from * 1 more time, ch 2, Shell St in last ch-3 sp. Turn.

**Row 12**: Work Beg Shell St in ch-3 sp, ch 1, Shell St in next ch-3 sp, ch 4, dc in top of next dc, ch 4, Shell St in next dc, ch 5, sc in ch 2 of ch-3 sp, Shell St in last ch-3 sp. Turn.

**Row 13**: Work Beg Shell St in ch-3 sp, ch 4, dc in top of next dc, ch 4, Shell St in next ch-3 sp, ch 4, dc in top of next dc, ch 5, sc in ch 2 of next ch-3 sp, Shell St in last ch-3 sp. Turn.

**Row 14**: Work Beg Shell St in ch-3 sp, ch 3, dc in top of next dc, ch 3, Shell St in next ch-3 sp, ch 3, dc in top of next dc, ch 3 Shell St in last ch-3 sp. Turn.

**Rows 15–23**: Rep Row 14.

*(continued next page)*

**Row 24 (shape neck)**: Work Beg Shell St in ch-3 sp, ch 3, dc in top of next dc, ch 3, Shell St in next ch-3 sp, ch 3, sc in top of next dc, sl st in next st. Fasten off.

## BACK

**Row 4**: Join yarn at 6th Shell St from right edge with RS facing. Work Beg Shell St in ch-3 sp, *ch 5, dc in top of next dc, ch 5, Shell St in next ch-3 sp; rep from * 5 times more. Turn.

**Row 5**: Work Beg Shell St in ch-3 sp, ch 4, *dc in top of next dc, ch 5, Shell St in next ch-3 sp, ch 5; rep from * 4 times more, dc in top of next dc, ch 4, Shell St in last ch-3 sp. Turn.

**Row 6**: Work Beg Shell St in ch-3 sp, ch 3, *dc in top of next dc, ch 5, Shell St in next ch-3 sp, ch 5; rep from * 4 times more, dc in top of next dc, ch 3, Shell St in last ch-3 sp. Turn.

**Row 7**: Work Beg Shell St in ch-3 sp, ch 2, *dc in top of next dc, ch 5, Shell St in next ch-3 sp, ch 5; rep from * 4 times more, dc in top of next dc, ch 2, Shell St in last ch-3 sp. Turn.

## DIVIDE FOR LEFT AND RIGHT BACKS

Right Back (RB) and Left Back (LB) are worked separately. In Row 8, they share the middle ch-3 sp in the Shell St. Cont instructions from this point for Right Back, beg on RS. After RB is finished, break yarn and reattach to LB on left armhole edge and proceed beg on WS.

**Row 8 (RB/RS)(LB/WS)**: Work Beg Shell St in ch-3 sp, ch 1, *dc in top of next dc, ch 4, Shell St in next ch-3 sp, ch 4; rep from * 1 time more, dc in top of next dc, ch 5, Shell St in next ch-3 sp. Turn.

**Row 9 (RB/WS) (LB/RS)**: Work Beg Shell St in ch-3 sp, *ch 4, dc in top of next dc, ch 4, Shell St in next ch-3 sp; rep from * 1 time more, ch 4, dc in top of next dc, Shell St in last ch-3 sp. Turn.

**Row 10**: Work Beg Shell St in ch-3 sp, dc in top of next dc, ch 3, *Shell St in next ch-3 sp, ch 4, dc in top of next dc, ch 4; rep from * 1 time more, Shell St in next ch-3 sp.

**Row 11**: Work Beg Shell St in ch-3 sp, *ch 4, dc in top of next dc, ch 4, Shell St in next ch-3 sp; rep from * 1 time more, ch 3, Shell St in next ch-3 sp.

**Row 12**: Work Beg Shell St in ch-3 sp, ch 2, *Shell St in next ch-3 sp, ch 4, dc in top of next dc, ch 4; rep from * 1 time more, Shell St in next ch-3 sp. Turn.

**Row 13**: Work Beg Shell St in ch-3 sp, *ch 4, dc in top of next dc, ch 4, Shell St in next ch-3 sp; rep from * 1 time more, Shell St in next ch-3 sp. Turn.

**Row 14**: Work Beg Shell St in ch-3 sp, sc in next ch-3 sp, *ch 4, dc in top of next dc, ch 4, Shell St in next ch-3 sp; rep from * 1 time more. Turn.

**Row 15**: Work Beg Shell St in ch-3 sp, *ch 4, dc in top of next dc, ch 4, Shell St in next ch-3 sp; rep from * 1 time more. Turn.

**Row 16**: Rep Row 15.

**Row 17**: Work Beg Shell St in ch-3 sp, *ch 3, dc in top of next dc, ch 3, Shell St in next ch-3 sp; rep from * 1 time more.

**Rows 18–23**: Rep Row 17.

**Row 24 (shape neck)**: Sl st through Shell St and ch 3 to 1st dc, sc in top of dc, ch 3, Shell St in next ch-3 sp, ch 3, dc in dc, ch 3, Shell St in last ch-3 sp.

With RS together, sew shoulders using a crochet seam. Weave in ends.

## SKIRTING

**Row 1**: With garment held upside down, join yarn at bottom right corner of medallion strip. Dc in every st across. Turn.

**Row 2 (RS) foundation row for skirting**: Work Beg Shell St in top of 1st dc, ch 5, *skip 4–6 dc, dc in top of next dc, ch 5, skip 4–6 dc, Shell St in top of next dc; rep from * across row. Turn.

**Note:** It's important to match vertical rows already established in upper garment bodice; therefore, the amount of skipped dcs may vary from 4 to 6, depending on vertical row placements above medallions.

***Row 3***: Work Beg Shell St in ch-3 sp, *
ch 5, dc in top of next dc, ch 5,
Shell St in next ch-3 sp; rep from *
to end. Turn.

***Rows 4–8***: Rep Row 3.

***Row 9 (inc row)***: Work Beg Shell St in
ch-3 sp, *ch 6, dc in top of next dc,
ch 6, Shell St in next ch-3 sp; rep
from * to end. Turn.

***Rows 10–20***: Rep Row 9.

***Row 21 (inc row)***: Work Beg Shell St
in ch-3 sp, *ch 7, dc in top of next
dc, ch 7, Shell St in next ch-3 sp, rep
from * to end. Turn.

***Rows 22–27***: Rep Row 21. Fasten off
and weave in ends.

## SIDE BORDER ON MEDALLION STRIP

Join yarn in top of last dc of upper row of
dcs above row of circles.

Sc in every st, ending in top of last dc of
row of dcs under medallion strip.

Rep for other front edge.

## DRAWSTRING

Ch 275.

***Row 1***: Sc in every ch across. Fasten off.

Weave in yarn ends.

Thread drawstring through row of circles.

*Designer:* **Mary Jane Hall**

82

Bench by Kimberli Matin, www.weldingmetalar

Victoria Secret's Angels may be the current symbol of boudoir beauty, but it's the 1920s that freed women of painful corsets and ugly undies. This cashmere and merino bobbled scarf mimics the long strands of pearls worn by flappers.

## Size
One Size Fits All

## Finished Measurements
Approx 3½"x 81"/9cm x 206cm

## You Will Need
Debbie Bliss Cashmerino Superchunky (55% merino wool, 33% microfiber, 12% cashmere; 3.5oz/100g = 82yd/75m): 4 skeins, color #16006—approx 328yd/300m of bulky-weight yarn, ⑤

Hook: 9mm/N-13 or size needed to obtain gauge

Small piece of cardboard or pom-pom maker

3 stitch markers

Yarn needle

## Stitches Used
Chain (ch)
Single crochet (sc)
Double crochet (dc)
Slip st (sl st)
Puff Stitch *(see below)*

## Gauge
*Take time to check your gauge.*
8 sc = 4"/10cm

## Pattern Stitch: Puff Stitch
Pull up loop to approx 1"/3cm. Keeping loop 1"/3cm from edge of row, (yo, keeping both loops on hook with middle finger, insert hook in same st and pull up to 1"/3cm again) 5 times; yo and pull yarn through all 11 loops on hook, ch 1 to secure.

## SCARF
Loosely ch 135 (for a longer or shorter scarf, use multiples of 3 + 1 on beg ch).

*Row 1:* Sc in 2nd ch from hook and in each ch across, turn (134 sc).

*Row 2:* Ch 3 (counts as 1st dc), dc in each sc across, ch 1 turn (134 dc).

*Row 3:* Sc in each dc, ch 1, turn (134 sc).

*Row 4:* Sl st in 1st 2 sc, *in same sp as last sl st, work Puff Stitch, sl st in each of next 3 sc; rep from * ending with sl st in corner st, fasten off (45 Puff sts).

*Note:* You should have 2 sl sts between each Puff st.

*(continued next page)*

With RS facing, join yarn to 1st ch at far right, on opposite side of scarf. Pull up loop on hook to 1"/3cm and rep Row 4 from *, ending with sl st in last ch (45 Puff sts).

*Note:* Sts will be worked into ch instead of sc.

To attach Puff sts to center dc row of scarf, begin at far right with RS facing.

Join yarn with sl st around 1st horizontal dc post, sl st around next 2 dc posts, ch 1, *work Puff Stitch in same sp, ch 1, sl st around next 3 dc posts, ch 1; rep from * across. After last Puff st is worked, end with sl st around last 2 dc, ch 1 to secure. Fasten off.

## NECK AREA
### (3 rows, worked on one side only)

The 6 long chs with pom-poms will be added to each corner of the neck section.

With RS facing, place marker at center of scarf between sts 67 and 68. Count over 14 sts to the left and place marker. Rep on right of center marker (28 sts from marker to marker). Join yarn to st at far right where marker was placed. Sc in same sp as sl st, and in each st over to left marker (27 sc). You should have 1 sc to right of 1st Puff st (at neck area) and 1 sc to left of 9th Puff st, 1 sc at back of each Puff st and 2 sc between each Puff st. Ch 1, turn.

*Next row*: Sc in each sc across, ch 1, turn (27 sc).

*Next row*: Skip 1st 2 sc, sl st in next 2 sc (3rd and 4th sts), *work Puff Stitch in same st as sl st, ch 1, sl st in next 3 sc; rep from * to last Puff st. After working 8th Puff st, sl st in last 2 sc (8 Puff sts). Fasten off.

## CHAINS AND POMPOMS
### Short center chain

With RS facing, join yarn to st at far right corner of neck. Ch 36 tightly, fasten off.

### Right chain

Join yarn to st at right of short center chain, ch 42 tightly, fasten off.

### Left chain

Join yarn to st at left of short center chain, ch 45 tightly, fasten off.

Three chains at left side of neck: Rep same as before, reversing number of chs (45 chs to right of center ch, and 42 chs to left of center ch).

### Small Pompoms (Make 6)

Take a ½"/1cm wide piece of cardboard (or use pompom maker) and tie the yarn around it with a knot. Slip a 10"/25cm piece of yarn (which will be the piece that secures the pompom together when finished) through the yarn that has been tied to the cardboard. Wrap the yarn tightly around the cardboard 85 times. Before taking yarn off cardboard, tie ends of 10"/25cm piece together tightly to secure. Take yarn off and cut loops at bottom, opposite tied end. Trim pompom to approx 2"/5cm.

### Large Pompoms

Make large pompoms in same manner as small pompoms, using a 2"/5cm wide piece of cardboard. For loose pompom, wrap 105 times. For fuller and tighter pompom, wrap 150 times.

### FINISH

Attach pompoms to ends of chains and ends of scarf. Weave in ends.

Kevork Djansezian/Associated Press

Chris Pizzello/Associated Press

★ **STARLETS** ★

*Designer:* **Whitney Larson**

*You can tell a lot about a woman by the boots she wears. This pair celebrates Jane Smith, the on-screen assassin whose black beauties almost blew her suburban cover.*

LEVEL: **INTERMEDIATE**

### Size
Shown in size 7½/38 shoe

### Finished Measurements
Circumference: 8–9"/20–23cm
   around the top of the boot,
   depending on st count
Length: Approx 18"/46cm
   (from top of heel)

### You Will Need
Karabella SuperYak (50% yak,
   50% merino; 1.75oz/50g =
   125yd/114m): 3 skeins, color
   Dark Charcoal #10158—approx
   375yd/342m of bulky-weight
   yarn, ⑤
Hooks: 3.25mm/D-3 and 4mm/
   G-6 or size to obtain gauge
Dress shoes with room to
   drill around the edge
   (pumps are ideal)

Drill with ⅛" drill bit
Yarn needle
4 stitch markers

### Stitches Used
Chain (ch)
Single crochet (sc)
Double crochet (dc)
Slip stitch (sl st)

### Gauge
*Take time to check your gauge.*
18 sc = 4"/10cm using
   smaller hook
14 rows = 4"/10cm using
   smaller hook

## DRILL
Drill holes, starting in the front of the shoe, every ½" around, slightly above sole. (Do not drill into seams.)

*Note:* The designer used the flat handle of a wooden spoon (approx ½" wide) to gauge where to drill. She did not mark the shoe, but you can do that. You can also tape around the shoe to get an idea of the height at which to drill, or you can simply eyeball it. You should expect 45–50 holes in a size 7½/38 shoe of the style mentioned in this pattern.

## BASE CHAIN
With smaller hook, insert hook from outside of shoe to inside, through 1st hole. Holding yarn on inside of shoe, pull up a loop of yarn through the hole to the outside. Insert hook in next hole, pull up a loop and pull new loop through loop on hook. A foundation chain will form around the base of the shoe. Work around as established, join last loop to 1st chain, fasten off, pull tail to inside of shoe, and secure.

## BOTTOM EDGE

*Note:* These two rows will be worked with the shoe upside down, giving an "edge" to cover the very bottom of the shoe under the foundation chain.

*Row 1*: Join yarn at chain at the back of the shoe. With smaller hook, ch 2 and sc around, working 2 sc in same ch as needed to cover shoe completely.

*Row 2*: Ch 3 and dc around. Bind off.

## SHOE

*Note:* The remaining rows are worked with the shoe right-side up, creating the shoe section and then the leg that forms the boot.

*Row 1*: Join yarn at chain at the back of the shoe. Ch 2, sc around, sl st to ch.

*Row 2*: Ch 2, sc around, sl st to ch.

*Row 3*: Place st markers on either side of front 5 sts. Ch 2, sc around, working sc2tog at each marker (2 sts dec), sl st to ch.

*Rows 4–6*: Place st markers on either side of front 7 sts. Ch 2, sc around, working sc2tog twice at each marker (4 sts dec), sl st to ch.

*Rows 7–8*: Rep Row 3.

*Rows 9–10*: Rep Row 4, adjusting dec as needed to keep yarn snug, but not tight, around shoe. At this point, work should cover the shoe and measure approx 3"/8cm from foundation chain; work more rows if needed (approx 40–45 sts, depending on shoe size).

*Row 11*: Place st markers on either side of front 12 sts. Ch 2, sc in same st, ch 3, skip 12 sts, sc around, sl st to beg ch (forming keyhole opening).

## LEG

*Row 1*: With larger hook, ch 3, dc in each sc and middle ch 3 around. Sl st to beg ch.

*Row 2*: Ch 3, dc around.

*Rows 3–9*: Place st markers on either side of middle 5 sts in front *and* back of shoe. Ch 3, dc to front st marker, dc2tog, dc, dc2tog (2 sts dec). Dc to back st marker, work 2 dc in next st, 3 dc, 2 dc in next st (2 sts inc), sl st to beg ch.

*Rows 10–23*: Ch 3, dc around. Sl st to beg ch.

*Row 24*: Sl st around the boot top.

## FINISH

With a yarn needle, weave in ends.

Work second shoe same as first.

# Gwyneth

Designer: **Vickie Howell**

## Size
One Size Fits All

## Finished Measurements
Ascot neck circumference:
14¼"/36cm or desired size

Cuff wrist circumference: 6"/15cm
or desired size

## You Will Need
Karabella Gossamer (30% kid
mohair, 52% nylon, 18%
polyester; 1.75oz/50g = 220yd/
200m): 2 skeins, color #6300—
approx 440yd/400m of DK-
weight yarn, (3)

Hooks: 4mm/G-6 and 5mm/H-8 or
size needed to obtain gauge

Yarn needle

6 vintage rhinestone buttons,
¼"/6mm in diameter

Sewing needle and thread

## Stitches Used
Chain (ch)

Single crochet (sc)

Double crochet (dc)

Treble crochet (tr)

Slip stitch (sl st)

## Gauge
*Take time to check your gauge.*

20 sc = 4"/10cm using double
strand and smaller hook

12 rows = 4"/10cm using double
strand and smaller hook

Romantic glamour is
guaranteed with ruffled
ascot and cuffs. From
office party to movie
awards, their luxurious
layers will turn heads.

# ASCOT

### NECKBAND
With smaller hook and double strand of
yarn, ch 9.

***Row 1***: Sc in 2nd ch from hook and to
end, turn.

***Row 2***: Ch 1, sc across, turn.

Rep Row 2 until neckband measures
14"/36cm or about ¼–½"/6mm–1cm
shorter than desired length.

***Buttonhole row***: Sl st, sc, ch 4, skip 1,
3 sc, ch 4, skip 1, sc, sl st. Fasten off.

### TOP TIER RUFFLE
Measure about 4"/10cm (adjust as necessary if you've lengthened your version)
from the right end of the neckband.

***Row 1***: With larger hook, pick up a st
and ch 2, *[3 tr, ch 1, 3 tr] in next st,
sc; rep from * 6 times more, ensuring
that last group of sts is evenly spaced
from opposite end of neckband. Turn.

***Rows 2–4***: Ch 3, dc in next st and every
st to end. Fasten off.

*(continued next page)*

## SECOND TIER RUFFLE

Flip up the top tier ruffle. Using smaller hook, pick up a st and work sts on the neckband on the same row that you did for the ruffle, starting about 1"/3cm in from the outer edge of the first ruffle.

*Row 1*: Ch 2, sc in next st 17 sts. Turn.

*Row 2*: Ch 2, sc to end.

*Rows 3–4*: Rep Row 2.

*Row 5*: Switch to larger hook. Ch 4, [2 tr, ch 1, 3 tr] in next st, sc, *[3 tr, ch 1, 3 tr] in next st, sc; rep from * 5 times more. Turn.

*Rows 6–8*: Ch 3, dc in next st and to end.

Fasten off.

## THIRD TIER RUFFLE

Flip up 2nd ruffle. With smaller hook, pick up a st at the point on the 2nd ruffle where the rows of sc stopped and the ruffle started. Rep instructions for Second Tier Ruffle.

## FINISH

Weave in ends. Sew on buttons to neckband end and as a decorative addition to neckband center.

## CUFFS

### MAKE 2

Using smaller hook and double strand of yarn, ch 31.

*Row 1*: Sc in 2nd ch from hook and to end, turn (30 sc).

*Row 2*: Ch 1, sc across, turn.

*Rows 3–5*: Rep Row 2.

*Row 6*: Ch 2, *[3 tr, ch 1, 3 tr] in next st, skip 1, sc, skip 1; rep from * 4 times more, sc to end, turn.

*Rows 7–8*: Ch 3, dc to end. Turn.

*Row 9*: Ch 2, sc to end. Fasten off.

### FINISH

Using smaller hook, pick up st at center of shorter edge of the cuffs band.

*Buttonhole row*: Ch 6, sl st in same place. Fasten off.

Weave in ends.

Sew button onto opposite end of cuff band (on longer tab).

*Designer:* **Vickie Howell**

STARLETS ★ *Mary-Kate*

93

## Size

Women's S/M

## Finished Measurements

Beret: Fits up to 22"/56cm head
Gloves: Fit approx 7"/18cm wrist

## You Will Need

SWTC Vickie Howell Collection
    Vegas (67% wool, 29% Soysilk,
    4% Lurex; 1.75oz/50g = 109yd/
    99m): 2 skeins, color Casino
    #418 for gloves, 2 skeins, color
    Casino #418 for beret version A
    *or* 2 skeins, color Martini #421
    for beret version B—approx
    436yd/396m of worsted-weight
    yarn, (4️⃣)

Hooks: 4mm/G-6 for gloves and
    6mm/J-10 for beret or size
    needed to obtain gauge

Yarn needle

## Stitches Used

Chain (ch)

Single crochet (sc)

Half double crochet (hdc)

Double crochet (dc)

Treble crochet (tr)

Slip stitch (sl st)

## Gauge

*Take time to check your gauge.*

Beret: 1- 3 tr cluster = 1½"/4cm
    using larger hook with yarn
    held doubled

Gloves: 16 sc = 4"/10cm

20 rows = 4"/10cm

Hollywood's hottest young fashion plates are donning berets and fingerless gloves for looks that range from boho-chic to vintage sophisticate. This version gets glam with a hint of glitter.

## BERET

With yarn held doubled and larger hook, ch 49. Join rnd with a sl st.

*Rnds 1–2*: Ch 1, sc to end of rnd, join.

*Rnd 3*: Ch 4 (counts as 1st tr), 2 tr in base of ch, *ch 3, skip 3, 3 tr in same st (3 tr cluster made); rep from * around, ending with ch 3, join in 3rd ch of ch-4.

*Rnd 4*: Ch 7 (counts as ch 3 and 1st tr), skip 1st 3 tr cluster, 3 tr in ch sp, *ch 3, skip cluster, 3 tr in ch sp; rep from * around, ending with 2 tr, join in 4th ch of ch-7.

*Rnd 5*: Ch 8 (counts as ch 4 and 1st tr), skip 1st cluster, 4 tr in ch sp, *ch 4, skip cluster, 4 tr; rep from * around, ending with 3 tr, join.

*Rnd 6*: Rep Rnd 3.

*Rnd 7*: Ch 7 (counts as ch 3 and 1st tr), skip cluster, *2 tr, ch 3, skip cluster,

2 tr; rep from * around, ending with 1 tr, join.

*Rnd 8*: Ch 6 (counts as ch 2 and 1st tr), skip cluster, 2 tr in ch sp, *ch 2, skip cluster, 2 tr; rep from * around, ending with 1 tr, join.

*Rnd 9*: Ch 4 (counts as 1st tr), *skip cluster, 2 tr; rep from * around, ending with 1 tr, join.

*Rnd 10*: Ch 3 (counts as 1st dc), dc in same sp, *2 dc in sp between last row's clusters; rep from * around, join.

*Rnd 11*: Ch 1, *sc2tog; rep from * around, join.

*Rnd 12*: Ch 4, 2 tr in base of ch. Fasten off.

## FINISH

Using yarn needle, sew flap down to close top off. Weave in ends.

# GLOVES

## LEFT HAND

### Loop Stitch Cuff

With single strand of yarn and smaller hook, ch 27.

*Row 1*: Sc in 2nd ch from hook and across. Turn.

*Row 2 (RS)*: *Ch 5, sc in front loop *only* of next st; rep from * to end. Turn.

*Row 3*: Ch 1, sc in back loop of *same* sts worked on the previous row. Turn.

Rep Rows 2–3 until piece measures 2"/5cm.

### Hand

*Next row (RS)*: Ch 1, sc to end. Fold piece with RS out and join rnd with a sl st. Work in rnds from this point.

*Next rnd*: Ch 1, sc around, join.

Rep last rnd until piece measures 3½"/9cm from edge of cuff.

### Thumb Gusset

*Next rnd*: Ch 1, 6 sc, (2 sc in next st) twice, sc to end, join.

*Next rnd*: Ch 1, sc around, join.

*Next rnd*: Ch 1, 5 sc, 2 sc in next st, 2 sc, 2 sc in next st, sc to end, join.

*Next rnd*: Ch 1, sc in next st and around, join.

*Next rnd*: Ch 1, 4 sc, 2 sc in next st, 4 sc, 2 sc in next st, sc to end, join.

*Next rnd*: Ch 1, sc around, join.

*Next rnd*: Ch 1, 3 sc, 2 sc in next st, 6 sc, 2 sc in next st, sc to end, join.

*Next rnd*: Ch 1, sc around, join.

*Next rnd*: Ch 1, 2 sc, 2 sc in next st, 8 sc, 2 sc in next st, sc to end, join.

*Next rnd*: Ch 1, sc around, join.

Rep last rnd until piece measures 7"/18cm, fasten off.

## RIGHT HAND

Work as for Left Hand to thumb shaping.

### Thumb Gusset

*Next rnd*: Ch 1, 21 sc, (2 sc in next st) twice, sc to end, join.

*Next rnd*: Ch 1, sc around, join.

*Next rnd*: Ch 1, 20 sc, 2 sc in next st, 2 sc, 2 sc in next st, sc to end, join.

*Next rnd*: Ch 1, sc in next st and around, join.

*Next rnd*: Ch 1, 19 sc, 2 sc in next st, 4 sc, 2 sc in next st, sc to end, join.

*Next rnd*: Ch 1, sc around, join.

*Next rnd*: Ch 1, 18 sc, 2 sc in next st, 6 sc, 2 sc in next st, sc to end, join.

*Next rnd*: Ch 1, sc around, join.

*Next rnd*: Ch 1, 17 sc, 2 sc in next st, 8 sc, 2 sc in next st, sc to end, join.

*Next rnd*: Ch 1, sc around, join.

Rep last rnd until piece measures 7"/18cm, fasten off.

## Thumbs

With glove facing palm down, measure 1¼"/3cm in from "thumb" edge. Pick up a st and ch 4, sl st across to same spot on opposite side of glove to create opening for thumb. Ch 2, hdc around thumb, join. Fasten off.

## FINISH

Rejoin yarn at palm end and ch 2, hdc around entire top edge. Fasten off. Weave in ends.

*Note:* The cuffs remain unseamed to make it easier to pull the gloves on and off.

Cameron

Designer: **Karen Baumer**

*From the malls of the O.C. to the beaches of Malibu, every California Girl needs a hoodie. Worked in small squares, this one's perfect for sun-kissed surfers hooking in the lulls between waves.*

## Size
S/M (L/XL, 2X/3X)

## Finished Measurements
Bust: 40(47, 55)"/102(119, 140)cm
Length: 20½(24¼, 28)"/52(62, 71)cm

## You Will Need
Knit Picks Shine Sport (60% Pima cotton, 40% Modal; 1.75oz/50g = 110yd/100m): (A), 5(6, 7) skeins, color Turquoise #23619; (B), 5(6, 7) skeins, color Sand #23620—approx 1100(1320, 1540) yd/1000(1200, 1400)m of sport-weight yarn, ②

Hook: 3.25mm/D-3(4mm/G-6, 5mm/H-8) or size needed to obtain gauge

Yarn needle

## Stitches Used
Chain (ch)
Single crochet (sc)
Double crochet (dc)
Slip stitch (sl st)

## Gauge
*Take time to check your gauge.*

1 square = 4(4¾, 5½)"/10(12, 14) cm with appropriate hook

**Note:** Instructions for all sizes are the same; the size difference is achieved by using different size hooks for each size.

## SQUARES (MAKE 49 IN A AND 48 IN B)
Ch 10. Join with sl st to form ring.

*Rnd 1:* Ch 2 (counts as 1st dc), 4 dc in ring, ch 9, *5 dc in ring, ch 9; rep from * 3 times total, end sl st into top of 1st ch 2.

*Rnd 2:* Ch 2 (counts as 1st dc), dc in next 2 dc, ch 2, dc in same sp as prev dc, dc in next 2 dc, ch 2, (3 dc, ch 5, 3 dc) in ch-9 sp, ch 2, *dc in next 3 dc, ch 2, dc in same sp as prev dc, dc in next 2 dc, ch 2, (3 dc, ch 5, 3 dc) in ch-9 sp, ch 2; rep from * around, end sl st into top of 1st ch 2 to join.

*(continued next page)*

**Rnd 3**: Ch 2, (yo, insert hook into next dc and pull up loop, yo, pull yarn through 1st 2 loops on hook) 5 times, yo and pull yarn through 6 loops on hook, *ch 5, dc in center dc of next set of 3 dc, ch 3, (2 dc, ch 2, 2 dc) in ch-5 sp, ch 3, dc in center dc of next set of 3 dc, ch 5, skip last dc of set where dc in center was just made, (yo, insert hook into next dc and pull up loop, yo, pull yarn through 1st 2 loops on hook) 6 times, yo and pull yarn through 7 loops on hook; rep from * around, end ch 5 and sl st into top of 1st cluster to join.

**Rnd 4**: Sc in each ch and each dc around, *except* work 2 dc in each 2-ch corner sp. Fasten off.

## HALF SQUARES
## (MAKE 2 IN A)

Ch 10. Join with sl st to form ring.

**Rnd 1**: Ch 11, 5 dc in ring, ch 9, 5 dc in ring, ch 11, sl st in ring.

**Rnd 2**: Ch 2, turn, (3 dc, ch 5, 3 dc) in ch-11 sp, *ch 2, dc in next 3 dc, ch 2, dc in same sp as prev dc, dc in next 2 dc, ch 2, (3 dc, ch 5, 3 dc) in ch-9 sp, rep from * working (3 dc, ch 5, 3 dc) in ch-11 sp, end ch 2, join with sl st in center ring.

**Rnd 3**: Ch 5, turn, *dc in middle dc of set of 3 dc, ch 3, (2 dc, ch 2, 2 dc) under next ch, ch 3, dc in middle dc of next set of 3, ch 5, skip last dc of set where dc in center was just made, (yo, insert hook into next dc and pull up loop, yo, pull yarn through 1st 2 loops on hook) 6 times, yo and pull

yarn through 7 loops on hook, ch 5, rep from *, end with dc in middle dc, ch 5 and join with sl st in center ring.

**Rnd 4**: Do not turn. Sc in each ch and each dc around, *except* work 2 dc in each 2-ch corner sp. Fasten off.

## FINISH
### Body Back

Make 3 strips of 5 turquoise squares and 2 strips of 5 sand squares. Sew together in stripes, starting and ending with a turquoise stripe.

### Body Front

Make 2 strips of 5 turquoise squares and 2 strips of 5 sand squares. Sew together in stripes, starting with a turquoise stripe (bottom) and ending with a sand stripe. Sew 1 turquoise square at upper right and upper left (shoulders), then sew in the 2 half-squares, one on each side, to form a modified V-neck. There is no center square on the top row of the front.

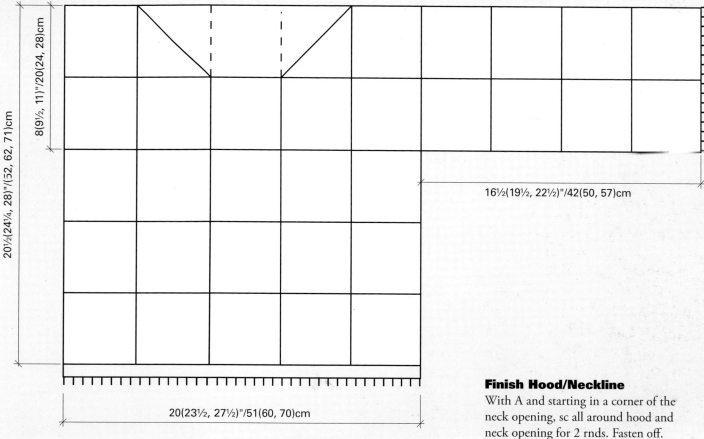

8(9½, 11)"/20(24, 28)cm

20½(24¼, 28)"/(52, 62, 71)cm

16½(19½, 22½)"/42(50, 57)cm

20(23½, 27½)"/51(60, 70)cm

## Sleeves (Make 2)

Make 2 strips each of 4 turquoise and 4 sand squares. Sew together in stripes. Bottom of sleeve is turquoise and top is sand.

## Hood

Make 2 strips of 6 sand squares and 1 strip of 6 turquoise squares. Sew together in stripes with turquoise strip in the middle.

Press all pieces with a steam iron and block to size. Sew shoulder seams. Attach hood to neckline, starting and ending at the bottom corners of the half-squares, easing to fit if necessary. Fold hood along center back and sew top seam of hood closed. Attach sleeves, centered at shoulder seams, sand stripe at top, then sew side and sleeve seams.

## Finish Hood/Neckline

With A and starting in a corner of the neck opening, sc all around hood and neck opening for 2 rnds. Fasten off.

## Finish Sleeve and Bottom

With A and starting at inner seam for sleeves and right side seam for bottom, sc all around for 2 rnds, then work 1 picot rnd as follows:

*Sc in next sc, ch 3, sl st in same st, sc in next 2 sc; rep from * to end of rnd and sl st to join, adjusting picot spacing slightly if necessary near the end of the rnd to achieve an even look. Fasten off.

*Designer:* **Vickie Howell**

## Size
Child's 4–10

## Finished Measurements
Neckline opening: 28"/71cm
Length (including edging):
   13"/33cm or desired length

## You Will Need
Moda Dea Curious (45% nylon,
   28% cotton, 27% acrylic; 1.75oz/
   50g = 78yd/71m): 3 skeins,
   color Mauve #9547—approx
   234yd/213m of bulky-weight
   yarn,
Hook: 6mm/J-10 or size needed
   to obtain gauge
16"/41cm chain with clasp
Stitch marker
Yarn needle

## Stitches Used
Chain (ch)
Single crochet (sc)
Half double crochet (hdc)
Double crochet (dc)
Slip stitch (sl st)

## Gauge
*Take time to check your gauge.*
10 dc = 4"/10cm
10 rows = 4"/10cm

**Note:** This piece is versatile and
   will fit a range of sizes.

Kiddie clothing mavens
like Miley Cyrus, Willow
Smith, and Ashley Tisdale
have instilled a fervor for
fashion in today's youth,
but it's Dakota Fanning
who best represents the
little girl-next-door. This
capelet celebrates being
cool without losing the kid.

## CAPELET BODY
Ch 70. Join rnd, being careful not to twist.

*Rnd 1*: Ch 1, sc around. Join with a sl st.

*Rnd 2*: Ch 2, hdc around. Join.

Rep Rnd 2 twice more.

*Next rnd*: Ch 3, dc around. Join.

Rep last rnd until piece measures
7"/18cm or 1½"/4cm less than desired
length. Join.

*Last rnd*: Ch 4, tr around. Join.
   Fasten off.

## NECKLACE LOOP
Find the top center of the front of capelet
and place a marker. With RS facing,
count 5 sts to the right of marker and
pick up a loop.

*Row 1*: Ch 1, sc in next 9 sts. Turn.

*Row 2*: Ch 1, sc across. Turn.

Rep Row 2 until piece measures 3"/8cm.
Fasten off.

## GARLAND EDGING
Pick up a loop at any point on the
bottom edge. *Ch 28, skip 20 sts or so
(the exact number of sts skipped doesn't
matter because this is supposed to look
freeform), sc. Rep around, not necessarily
worrying about making the skipped sps
the same length apart.

Fasten off.

Rep the process, only this time begin by
picking up a st in the center of one of
the skipped sps, chain, and then sc in the
next sp to create an overlapping effect.

## FINISH
Weave in ends. Fold necklace loop in half
and sew down. Insert chain through loop.

Drew

Designer: **Jennifer Hansen of Stitch Diva Studios**

## Size
One Size Fits All

## Finished Measurements
Approximately 3"/8cm in diameter

## You Will Need
2yd/2m gold wire, 28 gauge

15 teardrop, leaf, or flat triangle beads, approx 8mm x 18mm (A)

7 rice pearls, 6mm khaki green (B)

7 Swarovski crystals, 5mm amethyst (C)

1 glass teardrop bead, 3mm amethyst

1 eye pin, 1"/2.5cm gold

1 jump ring, 3mm gold

15"/38cm chain with clasp, gold

Hook: 1.65mm/7 steel crochet hook or size needed to obtain gauge

Hairpin lace frame

Round-nose pliers

## Stitches Used
Chain (ch)

Single crochet (sc)

## Gauge
Gauge is not important for this project.

*The free-spirited flower child of the '70s lives on in a masterfully designed Tunisian crochet pendant.*

## PROJECT NOTES

### MAKING LOOPS
Making loops with wire is easy with round-nose pliers. Using round-nose pliers, grab the wire at what will be the base of the loop. The larger the loop, the farther down on the wire you need to start the loop. Bend the wire to form a 90° angle. Be mindful when bending the wire of what plane you would like your loop to be in. Use the tapered nose of the round-nose pliers to control the size of the loop. Clamp the pliers down at the tip of the bent wire at the position on the nose that has the diameter loop that you desire. Twist the wire with the pliers to form the loop. It's helpful to leave a small space to connect the loop to another component. Once connected, use pliers to squeeze shut.

*(continued next page)*

## HAIRPIN LACE WITH WIRE

If necessary, search the web for in-depth hairpin lace instructions. This project assumes some familiarity with the technique.

• Width settings of adjustable hairpin looms vary between manufacturers. Try to use a loom that can get you to within ⅛"/3mm of the width settings called for in the pattern.

• Gauge for such a small project is not critical. Select hook size by aiming for a pleasing result.

• Count loops on both prongs of the loom when following pattern instructions.

• When working hairpin lace with wire, take the hook completely out of the stitch to turn the loom, then reinsert the hook once the loom is turned. This way, you'll avoid overworking the brittle wire.

### Working with Beads and Wire

• This pendant is created by catching the beads on each hairpin lace loop of the strip as it is worked. To start the strip, twist the wire into a loop around the prong, catching a bead in this loop. It will be easier to work if the bead is held to the back of the work.

• Prior to working the first stitch, bring the bead up to the front of the opposite prong, then work the stitch so that the second bead sits to the front of the loom.

• After working the next stitch, bring the bead to the stitch, then turn work. Repeat this step of bringing up a bead to each new stitch before turning loom.

• Work as many stitches as instructed, then fasten off work as usual. Notice that beads will be in a consistent position in relation to each prong. Placing the bead at each new stitch ensures that beads are always placed to the back of the loop that will be worked for the next stitch.

• When working with wire, you may need some new tools. You should have round-nose pliers, chain-nose pliers, wire cutters, and flat-nose pliers.

## MAKING THE PENDANT

### PRE-STRING BEADS

• This design requires pre-stringing beads. When you pre-string your wire with beads, string them in the reverse order that you will actually use them. This means that those you stitch with last are those to load onto the wire first. Although there are wonderful options for purchasing beads in local craft stores, at bead shows, and online, don't overlook the very best bead source: your own jewelry box! Take apart jewelry you no longer wear—this is not only the best type of recycling, but it also gives your new projects special meaning and history.

Pre-string beads in the following order: A (B, A, C, A) 7 times.

## WORK STRIP

Set loom to ½"/1cm and use a twisted loop on the starting prong instead of a slipknot, taking care that the 1st bead is caught in this 1st loop. Work 29 total loops with sc, catching a bead in each loop as it is made. Fasten off as usual. Leave 3"/8cm long beginning and ending tails.

## MAKE ROSETTE

Loops on one side of the strip will contain beads for the inside of the rosette, loops on the other side of the strip will contain beads for the outside "petals" of the rosette. Push beads for the inner side of the rosette to the same side of the loops (RS). Cut 6"/15cm of wire and run through loops holding the inner beads of the pendant. Twist ends of wire tightly on WS of pendant, causing the strip to curl upon itself into a circle. The circle should lay with the starting and ending sides of the strip adjacent to each other and with the inner loops of the strip forming a slight dome. Use the tails of the strip to weave the start and end of the strip together so that the strip now forms a continuous circle. Secure and trim all wire ends.

## MAKE PETALS

With fingers or flat-nose pliers, twist the wire holding the beads in the outer loops, being careful not to overtwist and break the wire.

## ATTACH CENTRAL BEAD

Cut a 6"/15cm length of wire and string a 3mm glass teardrop bead. Fold the wire in half and twist so that the bead is held on one end of the twisted wire. String the twisted wire ends through the center hole of the flower so that the width of the teardrop bead can't go through the center but is securely nestled on the RS of the work. Secure the ends of the wire at the WS of the flower.

## FINISH

Attach one side of the eye pin between the first and last petals of the rosette. Make a loop on the other side of the eye pin with pliers and connect it to the jump ring. String the rosette onto the chain through the jump ring.

Helena

Designer: **Vickie Howell**

Heeeeere's Helena! Ms. Bonham Carter embodies the dark, quirky beauty of cinematic thrillers and cult classics. In her honor, these crocheted mesh tops invite you to become entangled in the web where fright meets fashion. Redrum…

LEVEL: **BEGINNER**

## Size

S(M, L, XL, 2X, 3X)

*Stretches to fit blousy*

## Finished Measurements

Bust: 34(38, 42, 46, 50, 54)"/86(97, 107, 117, 127, 137)cm

Length: 29(29, 31, 33½, 34, 35)"/74(74, 79, 85, 86, 89)cm

## You Will Need

SWTC Vickie Howell Collection Love (70% bamboo, 30% silk; 1.75oz/50g = 99yd/90m): 10(11, 11, 12, 13, 14) skeins, color June & Johnny #255 or Sarah & Maurice #246—approx 990(1089, 1089, 1188, 1287, 1386)yd/900(990, 990, 1080, 1170, 1260)m of worsted-weight yarn, (**4**)

Small amount contrasting yarn for appliqué (optional)

Hooks: 4mm/G-6 and 5mm/H-8 or size needed to obtain gauge

Yarn needle

## Stitches Used

Chain (ch)

Single crochet (sc)

Half double crochet (hdc)

Slip stitch (sl st)

## Gauge

*Take time to check your gauge.*

28 sts = 4"/10cm in rib st using smaller hook

16 rows = 4"/10cm in rib st using smaller hook

4 st reps = 4"/10cm in pattern st using larger hook

**Note:** Make 2 of each element.

## RIBBED BAND

With smaller hook, ch 20. Sc in 2nd st from hook and in every chain in the row. Turn.

*Next row*: Ch 1, sc in front loop of 1st st and every st across row. Turn.

Rep last row until piece measures 16(18, 20, 22, 24, 26)"/41(46, 51, 56, 61, 66) cm. Fasten off.

## BODY

Switch to larger hook. Turn the band so it's facing horizontally and pick up a loop on the top right-hand corner. *Ch 5, skip 3, sc in next st; rep from * to end. Turn.

*Next row*: *Ch 5, skip 3, sc in next ch-5 sp; rep from * to end. Turn.

*(continued next page)*

Rep last row until piece measures 19(19, 20, 22, 22½, 23)"/48(48, 51, 56, 57, 58) cm from ribbed edge.

*Next row*: Ch 56(56, 60, 64, 68, 68) (for sleeve), sc in 8th ch from hook, *ch 5, skip 3, sc in next ch; rep from * to end of chain, complete row as established.

Rep last row for other sleeve.

*Next row*: *Ch 5, skip 3, sc in next ch-5 sp; rep from * to end. Turn.

Rep last row for 10(10, 11, 11½, 11½, 12)"/25(25, 28, 29, 29, 30)cm more.

*Next row*: Ch 1, sc in all ch and sc sts across row. Turn.

*Next row*: Ch 1, sc across. Turn.

Rep last row twice more. Fasten off.

Seam shoulders, leaving a 12"/30cm opening in the center for neck. Using whipstitch, seam up sides and sleeves.

## CUFFS

With larger hook, pick up loop at seam of sleeve edge. Sc around, join with sl st.

*Next row*: Ch 2, hdc around. Join.

Rep last row 4 times more. Fasten off.

Rep for 2nd sleeve.

## FINISH

Weave in ends, block if necessary.

## APPLIQUÉ (OPTIONAL)

With contrasting yarn, make a fun, funky freeform shape or try a motif from your favorite stitch dictionary. Sew in place on tunic, adding sequins if desired for extra glitz!

Designer: **Karen Baumer**

109

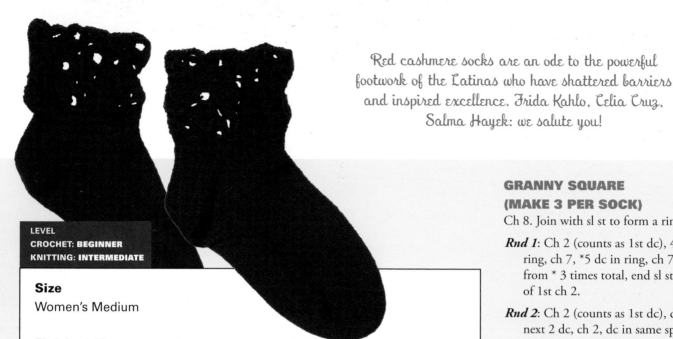

*Red cashmere socks are an ode to the powerful footwork of the Latinas who have shattered barriers and inspired excellence. Frida Kahlo, Celia Cruz, Salma Hayek: we salute you!*

## Size
Women's Medium

## Finished Measurements
Circumference: 8"/20cm
Foot length: 8¾"/22cm or
    desired length

## You Will Need
Karabella Supercashmere Fine
    (100% cashmere; 0.88oz/25g =
    202yd/187m): 2 skeins, color Deep
    Red #5095—approx 404yd/368m
    of fingering-weight yarn, **①**
Hook: 2.25mm/B-1 or size needed to
    obtain gauge
Knitting needles: 2.25mm/US1
    double pointed, set of 5 or size
    needed to obtain gauge
Yarn needle
Stitch markers (optional)

## Stitches Used
Chain (ch)
Single crochet (sc)
Double crochet (dc)
Slip stitch (sl st)
Knit (k)
Purl (p)
Stockinette stitch (St st)

## Crochet Gauge
*Take time to check your gauge.*
1 granny square = 2.75"/7cm

## Knit Gauge
*Take time to check your gauge.*
34 sts x 48 rows = 4"/10cm in St st

## GRANNY SQUARE (MAKE 3 PER SOCK)

Ch 8. Join with sl st to form a ring.

*Rnd 1*: Ch 2 (counts as 1st dc), 4 dc in ring, ch 7, *5 dc in ring, ch 7; rep from * 3 times total, end sl st into top of 1st ch 2.

*Rnd 2*: Ch 2 (counts as 1st dc), dc in next 2 dc, ch 2, dc in same sp as prev dc, dc in next 2 dc, ch 2, (3 dc, ch 5, 3 dc) in ch-7 sp, ch 2, *dc in next 3 dc, ch 2, dc in same sp as prev dc, dc in next 2 dc, ch 2, (3 dc, ch 5, 3 dc) in ch-7 sp, ch 2; rep from * around, end sl st into top of 1st ch 2 to join.

*Rnd 3*: Ch 2, (yo, insert hook into next dc and pull up loop, yo, pull yarn through 1st 2 loops on hook) 5 times, yo and pull yarn through 6 loops on hook, *ch 5, dc in center dc of next set of 3 dc, ch 3, (2 dc, ch 2, 2 dc) in ch-5 sp, ch 3, dc in center dc of next set of 3 dc, ch 5, skip last dc of set where you just made a dc in center, (yo, insert hook into next dc and pull up loop, yo, pull yarn through 1st 2 loops on hook) 6 times, yo and pull yarn through 7 loops on hook; rep from * around, end ch 5 and sl st into top of 1st cluster to join.

**Rnd 4**: Sc in each ch and each dc around, *except* work 2 dc in each ch-2 corner sp. Fasten off.

Sew squares together to form a cuff.

## FOOT

With dpns, pick up 68 sts evenly spaced around bottom edge of cuff, starting at one seam and placing 17 sts on each of 4 needles. (It is helpful to put a st marker at back seam and additional markers at each quarter point to facilitate picking up sts evenly.) Working in the rnd, knit 7 rows.

## HEEL FLAP

**Set up row 1 (RS)**: K17, turn.

**Set up row 2 (WS)**: Sl 1, p33, turn.

(One cuff seam should be centered over heel flap sts.)

Working back and forth on 2 needles over these 34 sts only, work heel flap as follows:

**Row 1 (RS)**: *[Sl 1, k1]; rep from * across.

**Row 2 (WS)**: Sl 1, p to end.

Rep these 2 rows 18 times for a total of 36 rows, then work Row 1 one more time, ending with WS facing.

## TURN HEEL

**Row 1 (WS)**: Sl 1, p17, p2tog, p1, turn.

**Row 2 (RS)**: Sl 1, k3, ssk, k1, turn.

**Row 3**: Sl 1, p4, p2tog, p1, turn.

**Row 4**: Sl 1, k5, ssk, k1, turn.

**Row 5**: Sl 1, p6, p2tog, p1, turn.

**Row 6**: Sl 1, k7, ssk, k1, turn.

Proceed in this fashion, increasing by 1 the number of sts worked before the dec in each row, until all of the sts have been worked, finishing with a RS row (18 sts rem).

Divide the 18 heel sts evenly on 2 needles. With RS facing, use the needle on the side where yarn is joined to pick up 18 sts along the slipped st edge of the heel flap— 1 st per sl st plus 1 in the "corner" just before live sts begin (needle 1). Knit in the usual fashion across instep sts (needles 2 and 3). With empty needle, pick up 18 sts down side of heel flap to match other side, k9 rem heel sts (needle 4) (86 sts).

## GUSSET

**Rnd 1**: K9, k18 tbl, k34, k18 tbl, k9.

**Rnd 2**: K until 3 sts rem on needle 1, k2tog, k1; k across needles 2 and 3; on needle 4, k1, ssk, k to end.

**Rnd 3**: Knit.

Rep Rnds 2 and 3 only until 68 sts rem (17 sts per needle).

Cont even in St st until foot measures 7"/18cm from back of heel, or 1¾"/4cm less than desired length.

## TOE

**Rnd 1**: On needle 1, k to last 3 sts, k2tog, k1; on needle 2, k1, ssk, k to end; on needle 3, k to last 3 sts, k2tog, k1; on needle 4, k1, ssk, k to end.

**Rnd 2**: Knit.

Rep these 2 rnds until 32 sts rem, then rep Rnd 1 only until 12 sts rem. Break off yarn, leaving a 12"/30cm tail. Graft toe together using Kitchener stitch.

Weave in ends and block lightly, if needed.

Work second sock same as first.

Designer: **Edith Beumer Kemp**

★ STARLETS ★ *Sandra*

112

## Size

S(M, L)

## Finished Measurements

Low waist: 28(32, 37)"/71(81, 94)cm

Length: 31"/79cm or desired length

## You Will Need

SWTC Oasis (100% Soysilk; 3.5oz/100g = 240yd/218m): 7(8, 8) skeins, color Napa Valley #502—approx 1680(1920, 1920) yd/1526(1744, 1744)m of DK-weight yarn, ③

Hooks: 3.75mm/F-5, 4mm/G-6, 5mm/H-8, 6mm/J-10, 6.5mm/K-10.5, and 8mm/L-11 or size needed to obtain gauge

Petersham ribbon for waist stay, waist measurement plus 10"/25cm

7 large hooks and eyes

Commercial pattern for an A-line bias skirt

Rayon fabric for lining (refer to pattern for quantity)

All-purpose sewing thread to match garment

## Stitches Used

Chain (ch)

Single crochet (sc)

Double crochet (dc)

Slip stitch (sl st)

## Pattern Stitches:

### Puff Stitch

*Yo, insert hook behind post of previous round's ch 2, yo and pull up a loop; rep from * twice more (7 loops on hook). Yo and pull through all 7 loops, close with sc.

### V-Stitch

Work (dc, ch 1, dc) in same st

### Gauge

*Take time to check your gauge.*

20 sc = 4"/10cm using smallest hook

*From ranch to restaurant, this convertible skirt or strapless dress makes for the perfect weekender wardrobe. When it comes to versatility, here's a project that offers Practical Magic.*

## SKIRT

With smallest hook, ch 140(160, 185). Turn, ch. 1, sc in each st.

Rep for 17 rows, ending with RS row. Join to beg of row with sl st.

***Next rnd (set up for Puff st):*** Ch 2, dc in 2nd st from hook, ch 1, dc in same st, *dc in next st, (dc, ch 1, dc) in next st; rep from * to end of rnd, join with sl st to beg ch 2.

Change to 4mm hook. *Yo, insert hook behind post of previous round's ch 2, yo and pull up a loop; rep from * twice more (7 loops on hook). Yo and pull through all 7 loops, close with sc (Puff st made), **(dc, ch 1, dc) in next ch-1 sp (V-st made), work puff st in next dc; rep from ** to end of rnd, ending with a V-st; join with sl st to top of 1st Puff st.

Cont as established, working 6 rnds with 4mm hook, 6 rnds with 5mm hook, 8 rnds with 6mm hook, 10 rnds with 6.5mm hook, and 19 rnds with 8mm hook to shape skirt to an A-line. For a

*(continued next page)*

shorter skirt, change hooks more frequently and stop at desired length.

### HEM

Make a Puff st behind each Puff st, Puff st behind 1st leg of V-st, dc in ch-1 sp of V-st, Puff st behind dc on 2nd leg of V-st.

Rep around and join to beg of rnd with sl st.

*Last rnd*: Make a Puff st behind each Puff st and post of prev rnd, join with sl st at end of rnd, fasten off.

### FINISH

To block, spray lightly with water and lay out on towel. Use rustproof pins to shape points along hem. Let dry. Cut steek (see box) as follows for placket: Sew 2 parallel rows of short, narrow zigzag sts on pattern st portion of skirt ¼"/6mm apart for 4"/10cm, aligned with waistband opening. Carefully cut between the lines of stitching. Join a single strand of yarn at top of steek and single crochet along both sides. Fasten off and weave in loose ends.

Cut lining from commercial pattern to match length of skirt. Leave left side seam open for 8"/20cm at top to allow for placket. Finish raw edges of placket, hem, and side seams. Press seams to one side. Press placket open. Put lining in place and baste top of lining to skirt ½"/1cm below upper edge of waistband.

Cut ribbon to fit around placket openings and top of waistband. Gently steam ribbon into a slight curve. Pin it along edges of placket openings and across waistband, mitering corners and folding under edges. Mark places for 4 hooks and eyes along placket openings. Sew along both edges of ribbon with small stitches, catching inside of crochet work and enclosing hooks and eyes beneath ribbon. Using a doubled thread, sew through ribbon and skirt to attach hooks and eyes in place. Sew 3 sets of hooks and eyes along crocheted placket area between the lining and the skirt.

A steek is a slit cut into the knitting after reinforcing the stitches on each side to prevent unraveling.

Kate

*Designer:* **Whitney Larson**

Kate Hudson has made bohemian-chic almost famous by wearing it in films and in her personal life. The look is at once grounded and eclectic. A crocheted capelet adds a pop of color and a splash of artsy to any outfit.

## Size
One Size Fits All

## Finished Measurements
Neck circumference: 14"/36cm (can be made larger by extending strap)

Length: 20"/51cm

## You Will Need
Berroco Softwist (59% rayon, 41% wool; 1.75oz/50g = 100yd/91m): 3 skeins, color Ginger #9418—approx 300yd/273m of worsted-weight yarn, (4)

Hook: 4mm/G-6 or size needed to obtain gauge

2 buttons, ¾"/2cm in diameter

Yarn needle

## Stitches Used
Chain (ch)

Single crochet (sc)

Slip stitch (sl st)

Afghan Stitch (see next column)

Knot Stitch (see column at right)

## Gauge
*Take time to check your gauge.*

18 sc = 4"/10cm

14 rows = 4"/10cm

## Pattern Stitches:
## Afghan Stitch
*Note:* For this pattern, you do not need an afghan hook.

### First Half of Foundation Row
Starting in the 1st ch from hook, insert hook in chain, yo and draw up a loop. Continue working across, drawing up a loop in each st of the chain. Leave all the loops on the hook. Now count the loops; there should be the same number of loops as number of starting chain.

### Second Half of Foundation Row
Working from left to right, yo and draw through 1 loop, *yo and draw through 2 loops; rep from * across until 1 loop rem on the hook.

This is the 1st st of the next row.

## Pattern Row
Skip the 1st upright bar, directly below the hook. Draw up a loop in each bar across. Leave all the loops on the hook; work off the loops in the same manner as the 2nd half of the foundation row. *Note:* When drawing up a loop on the last st of the row, insert hook through the entire st, not just under the bar. This makes a firm selvage edge.

## Knot Stitch
**Row 1:** Sc, draw up a 1"/3cm loop, yo and pull through loop on hook, insert hook between the 1"/3cm loop and the single strand behind it, draw a loop through (2 loops on hook), yo and pull through all loops on hook (knot st made); make another knot st, skip next 4 sts, sc in next st, (knot st loop made); rep from * across. Make 2 knot sts, turn.

**Row 2:** Sl st in center of 1st knot st loop; * work 2 knot sts, sl st in center of next loop, rep from * across. Make 2 knot sts, turn. Rep Row 2 for pattern.

## COLLAR

Ch 12.

Work in Afghan Stitch for 12"/30cm or desired length.

Turn, sc across, fasten off.

## COLLAR TAB

Ch 12.

*Rows 1–4*: Work in Afghan Stitch.

*Row 5 (buttonhole row)*: Ch 1, 3 sc, ch 2, skip 2 sts, 2 sc, ch 2, skip 2 sts, sc to end.

Work in Afghan Stitch for 1"/3cm more.

*Next row*: Ch 1, sc across.

## JOIN TAB TO COLLAR

*Row 1*: Ch 8, join with sl st to end of collar.

*Row 2*: Sl st across to the 4th st, ch 8, join with sl st to same st on collar tab (working back and forth from tab to collar).

*Row 3*: Sl st across to 8th st, ch 8, join with sl st to 8th st on collar.

*Row 4*: Sl st to last st, ch 4, wrap yarn around all chains, join with a sl st. Ch 4, join end of ch to last st on collar tab. Fasten off.

Join yarn at edge of collar tab, work 1 row of sc around edges of tab and top/sides of collar. Fasten off.

Block the collar by pressing with a hot iron and wet hand towel (now or when complete).

## CAPELET

*Row 1*: With RS facing, join yarn at bottom edge of long piece of collar, work 50 sc across. *Note*: If you made a longer or shorter collar, adjust stitch count as needed, being sure to end up with a multiple of 5 sts after Row 10.

*Row 2*: Sc across, increasing (work 2 sc in 1 st) every 5 sts (60 sts).

*Row 3*: Sc across, increasing every 5 sts (72 sts).

*Row 4*: Sc across, increasing every 6 sts (84 sts).

*Row 5*: Sc across, increasing every 6 sts (98 sts).

*Row 6*: Sc across, increasing every 7 sts (112 sts).

*Row 7*: Sc across, increasing every 7 sts (128 sts).

*Row 8*: Sc across, increasing every 8 sts (144 sts).

*Row 9*: Sc across, increasing every 8 sts (162 sts).

*Row 10*: Sc across, increasing every 9 sts (180 sts).

*Rows 11–29*: Work in Knot Stitch across.

Fasten off.

## FINISH

Block collar (if not done earlier).

Attach buttons opposite buttonholes.

# ★ ROCKERS ★

Tina Fineberg/
Associated Press

Steve Russell/ CP PHOTO/
Toronto Star/Associated Press

Bernhard Kristinn Ingimundarson/
The Icelandic Love Corporation, 2007

Designer: **Pam Gillette**

## Size

Women's S(M, L, XL)

## Finished Measurements

Bust: 32(36, 40, 44)"/
81(91, 102, 112)cm

Waist: 28(30, 32, 34)"/
71(76, 81, 86)cm

## You Will Need

Berroco Suede (100% nylon;
1.75oz/50g = 120yd/109m):
10(10, 12, 12) balls, color Zorro
#3729—approx 1200(1200, 1440,
1440)yd/1090(1090, 1308, 1308)m
of worsted-weight yarn, (4)

Hook: 6mm/J-10 or size needed
to obtain gauge

5(5, 6, 6) buttons, ½"/1cm
in diameter

Smaller hook for weaving in ends

Sewing needle and black thread

## Stitches Used

Chain (ch)

Half double crochet (hdc)

Double crochet (dc)

Slip stitch (sl st)

## Gauge

*Take time to check your gauge.*

12 hdc = 4"/10cm

8 rows = 4"/10cm

**Note:** Use 2 strands of yarn
throughout. Turning chain does
not count as st in this pattern.

Harley-Davidson style is tough
and sexy: sturdy boots, denim
jeans, leathers. Withstand the tests
of fashion (and of the road) in a
dainty version of a biker vest.

# FRONT PANEL

## MAKE 2

Start at point A and work up to B/E on
schematics diagram (page 123), increasing on both sides. Instructions here are
for all sizes.

*Row 1*: Ch 2, then work 2 dc in 2nd ch
from hook, ch 2 and turn.

*Row 2*: Work 2 dc in each st, ch 2 and
turn (4 sts).

*Row 3*: 4 hdc, ch 2 and turn (4 sts).

*Row 4*: 2 hdc in 1st st, 2 hdc, work 2 hdc
in last st, ch 2 and turn (6 sts).

*Row 5*: 2 hdc in 1st st, 4 hdc, work 2 hdc
in last st, ch 2 and turn (8 sts).

*Row 6*: 2 hdc in 1st st, 6 hdc, work 2 hdc
in last st, ch 2 and turn (10 sts).

*Row 7*: 2 hdc in 1st st, 8 hdc, work 2 hdc
in last st, ch 2 and turn (12 sts).

*Row 8*: 2 hdc in 1st st, 10 hdc, work 2
hdc in last st, ch 2 and turn (14 sts).

*Row 9*: 2 hdc in 1st st, 12 hdc, work 2
hdc in last st, ch 2 and turn (16 sts).

*Row 10*: 2 hdc in 1st st, 14 hdc, work 2
hdc in last st, ch 2 and turn (18 sts).

*Row 11*: 2 hdc in 1st st, 16 hdc, work 2
hdc in last st, ch 2 and turn (20 sts).

*Row 12*: 2 hdc in 1st st, 18 hdc, work 2
hdc in last st, ch 2 and turn (22 sts).

## SIZE ADJUSTMENTS

These begin after Row 12.

For Size S, crochet 4 rows of 22 hdc,
ch 2 and turn (22 sts), then skip to
**Front Panel Waist Shaping** Row 1.

For Sizes M, L, and XL, inc by working
2 hdc in 1st st, 22 hdc, inc by working
2 hdc in last st, ch 2, turn (24 sts), size
M cont to **Front Panel Additional Row
Adjustments before Waist Shaping**.

For Sizes L and XL, inc by working 2 hdc
in 1st st, 24 hdc, inc by working 2 hdc
in last st, ch 2, turn (26 sts), size L cont
to **Front Panel Additional Row Adjustments before Waist Shaping**.

For Size XL only, inc by working 2 hdc in 1st st, 26 hdc, inc by working 2 hdc in last st, ch 2, turn (28 sts), cont to **Front Panel Additional Row Adjustments before Waist Shaping**.

You have now finished Point A to B/E on the diagram.

## Front Panel Additional Row Adjustments before Waist Shaping

Medium: Add 3 additional rows of 24 hdc here, ch 2, turn.

Large: Add 2 additional rows of 26 hdc here, ch 2, turn.

XL: Add 1 additional row of 28 hdc here, ch 2, turn.

## Front Panel Waist Shaping

In this section, you dec on one side only, every other row.

*Row 1*: 20(22, 24, 26) hdc, dec by working last 2 hdc tog, ch 2, turn.

*Rows 2–4*: 21(23, 25, 27) hdc, ch 2, turn.

*Row 5*: 19(21, 23, 25) hdc, dec by working last 2 hdc tog, ch 2, turn.

*Row 6*: 20(22, 24, 26) hdc, ch 2, turn.

*Row 7*: 18(20, 22, 24) hdc, dec by working last 2 hdc tog, ch 2, turn.

*Rows 8–10*: 19(21, 23, 25) hdc, ch 2, turn.

## Front Panel Additional Row Adjustments before Bust Shaping

Large: Add 2 additional rows of 23 hdc here, ch 2, turn.

XL: Add 2 additional rows of 25 hdc here, ch 2, turn.

## FRONT PANEL BUST SHAPING

In this section, you inc on one side only, every other row.

*Row 1*: 19(21, 23, 25) hdc, inc by working 2 hdc in last st, ch 2, turn.

*Row 2*: 20(22, 24, 26) hdc, ch 2, turn.

*Row 3*: 20(22, 24, 26) hdc, inc by working 2 hdc in last st, ch 2, turn.

*Row 4*: 21(23, 25, 27) hdc, ch 2, turn.

*Row 5*: 21(23, 25, 27) hdc, inc by working 2 hdc in last st, ch 2, turn.

*Row 6*: 22(24, 26, 28) hdc, ch 2, turn.

*Row 7*: 22(24, 26, 28) hdc, inc by working 2 hdc in last st, ch 2, turn.

*Row 8*: 23(25, 27, 29) hdc, ch 2, turn.

*Row 9*: 23(25, 27, 29) hdc, inc by working 2 hdc in last st, ch 2, turn.

*Row 10*: 24(26, 28, 30) hdc, ch 2, turn.

Cont on with 8(8, 10, 10) rows of 24(26, 28, 30) hdc, ch 2, turn.

## FRONT PANEL STRAP

*Row 1*: Sl st 10(10, 11, 11), then 10 hdc, ch 2, (skipping rem sts) turn.

*Row 2*: Dec by working 1st 2 sts tog, hdc 6, dec by working last 2 sts tog, ch 2, turn.

*Row 3*: 6 hdc, dec by working last 2 sts tog (7 sts).

Now crochet 15(15, 16, 16) rows of 7 hdc, ch 2, turn—approx 7(7, 7½, 8)"/ 18(18, 19, 20)cm strap length. On last row of strap, leave a tail of yarn approx 6"/15cm to use to whipstitch the top of straps tog when fastening off.

## BACK PANEL

Start at A and work up to B/E on the diagram, increasing on both sides. Instructions here are for all sizes.

*Row 1*: Ch 2, then work 2 dc in 2nd ch from hook, ch 2 and turn.

*Row 2*: Work 2 dc in each st, ch 2 and turn (4 sts).

*Row 3*: 4 hdc, ch 2 and turn (4 sts).

*Row 4*: 2 hdc in 1st st, 2 hdc, work 2 hdc in last st, ch 2 and turn (6 sts).

*Row 5*: 2 hdc in 1st st, 4 hdc, work 2 hdc in last st, ch 2 and turn (8 sts).

*Row 6*: 2 hdc in 1st st, 6 hdc, work 2 hdc in last st, ch 2 and turn (10 sts).

*Row 7*: 2 hdc in 1st st, 8 hdc, work 2 hdc in last st, ch 2 and turn (12 sts).

*Row 8*: 2 hdc in 1st st, 10 hdc, work 2 hdc in last st, ch 2 and turn (14 sts).

*Row 9*: 2 hdc in 1st st, 12 hdc, work 2 hdc in last st, ch 2 and turn (16 sts).

*Row 10*: 2 hdc in 1st st, 14 hdc, work 2 hdc in last st, ch 2 and turn (18 sts).

*(continued next page)*

*Row 11*: 2 hdc in 1st st, 16 hdc, work 2 hdc in last st, ch 2 and turn (20 sts).

*Row 12*: 2 hdc in 1st st, 18 hdc, work 2 hdc in last st, ch 2 and turn (22 sts).

## SIZE ADJUSTMENTS

Begin adjusting for size after Row 12.

For Size S, crochet 4 rows of 22 hdc, ch 2 and turn (22 sts), fasten off and weave in ends.

For Sizes M, L, and XL, inc by working 2 hdc in 1st st, 22 hdc, inc by working 2 hdc in last st, ch 2, turn (24 sts), fasten off and weave in ends.

For Sizes L and XL, inc by working 2 hdc in 1st st, 24 hdc, inc by working 2 hdc in last st, ch 2, turn (26 sts), fasten off and weave in ends.

For Size XL only, inc by working 2 hdc in 1st st, 26 hdc, inc by working 2 hdc in last st, ch 2, turn (28 sts), fasten off and weave in ends.

You have now finished Point A to B/E on the diagram. Make 2nd point exactly the same, but don't fasten off yet, join points with sl st, at Point E on diagram, and fasten off, weave in ends.

Join yarn to either end of the 2 joined points, Point B on diagram, ch 2 and do 1 row of hdc (be careful not to lose the 2 sts at the sl st join; they tend to hide).

Size S cont to **Back Panel Waist Shaping** Row 1, for M, L, and XL cont to **Back Panel Additional Row Adjustments before Waist Shaping**.

## Back Panel Additional Row Adjustments before Waist Shaping

Medium: Add 3 additional rows of 48 hdc here, ch 2, turn.

Large: Add 2 additional rows of 52 hdc here, ch 2, turn.

XL: Add 1 additional row of 56 hdc here, ch 2, turn.

## Back Panel Waist Shaping

In this section, dec on both sides, every other row.

**Row 1:** Dec by working 1st 2 sts tog, hdc 40(44, 48, 52), dec by working last 2 hdc tog, ch 2, turn.

**Rows 2–4:** Hdc 42(46, 50, 54), ch 2, turn.

**Row 5:** Dec by working 1st 2 sts tog, 38(42, 46, 50) hdc, dec by working last 2 hdc tog, ch 2, turn.

**Row 6:** 40(44, 48, 52) hdc, ch 2, turn.

**Row 7:** Dec by working 1st 2 sts tog, 36(40, 44, 48) hdc, dec by working last 2 hdc tog, ch 2, turn.

**Rows 8–10:** 38(42, 46, 50) hdc, ch 2, turn.

## Back Panel Additional Row Adjustments before Bust Shaping

Large: Add 2 additional rows of 46 hdc here, ch 2, turn.

XL: Add 2 additional rows of 50 hdc here, ch 2, turn.

*(continued next page)*

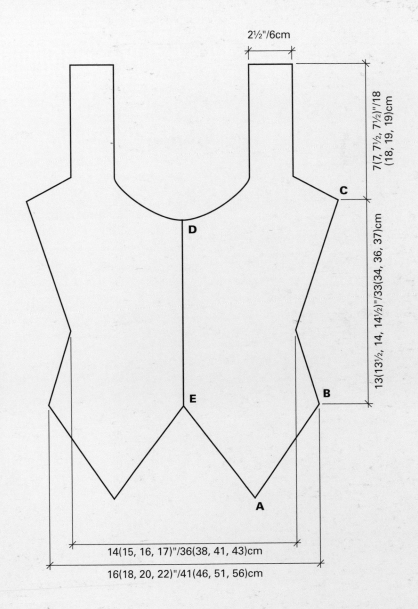

2½"/6cm

7(7, 7½, 7½)"/18 (18, 19)cm

13(13½, 14, 14½)"/33(34, 36, 37)cm

14(15, 16, 17)"/36(38, 41, 43)cm

16(18, 20, 22)"/41(46, 51, 56)cm

## BACK PANEL BUST SHAPING

In this section, inc on both sides, every other row.

*Row 1*: 2 hdc in 1st st, 38(42, 46, 50) hdc, then 2 hdc in last st, ch 2, turn.

*Row 2*: 40(44, 48, 52) hdc, ch 2, turn.

*Row 3*: 2 hdc in 1st st, 40(44, 48, 52) hdc, then 2 hdc in last st, ch 2, turn.

*Row 4*: 42(46, 50, 54) hdc, ch 2, turn.

*Row 5*: 2 hdc in 1st st, 42(46, 50, 54) hdc then 2 hdc in last st, ch 2, turn.

*Row 6*: 44(48, 52, 56) hdc, ch 2, turn.

*Row 7*: 2 hdc in 1st st, 44(48, 52, 56) hdc then 2 hdc in last st, ch 2, turn.

*Row 8*: 46(50, 54, 58) hdc, ch 2, turn.

*Row 9*: 2 hdc in 1st st, 46(50, 54, 58) hdc then 2 hdc in last st, ch 2, turn.

*Row 10*: 48(52, 56, 60) hdc, ch 2, turn.

Cont with 8(8, 10, 10) rows of 48(52, 56, 60) hdc, ch 2, turn.

(On last row, omit turning ch, as you will begin next row with a sl st.)

## BACK PANEL 1ST STRAP

*Row 1*: Sl st 1(10, 11, 11) then 10 hdc, ch 2, turn (skip rem sts).

*Row 2*: Dec by working 1st 2 sts tog, 6 hdc, dec by working last 2 sts tog, ch 2, turn.

*Row 3*: 6 hdc, dec by working last 2 sts tog (7 sts).

Now crochet 15(15, 16, 16) rows of 7 hdc, ch 2, turn—approx 7(7, 7½, 8)"/18(18, 19, 20)cm strap length. On last row of strap, leave a tail of yarn approx 6"/15cm to use to whipstitch the top of straps tog when fastening off.

## BACK PANEL 2ND STRAP

For the other strap, join yarn 10(10, 11, 11) sts in, to opposite end of complete strap.

*Row 1*: Ch 2, hdc 10, ch 2, turn.

*Row 2*: Dec by working 1st 2 sts tog, 6 hdc, dec by working last 2 sts tog, ch 2, turn.

*Row 3*: 6 hdc, dec by working last 2 sts tog (7 sts).

Now crochet 15(15, 16, 17) rows of 7 hdc, ch 2, turn—approx 7(7, 7½, 8)"/18(18, 19, 20)cm strap length. On last row of strap, leave a tail of yarn approx 6"/15cm to use to whipstitch the top of straps tog when fastening off.

## BUTTONHOLE ROW

One Front Panel needs a row for buttonholes; on the other Front Panel, you sew on buttons. For one Front Panel only, starting at Point D to Point E according to diagram, join yarn, ch 2, hdc 1, *ch 1, (for buttonhole) skip 1 st, hdc 5; rep from * across for a total of 5(5, 6, 6) buttonholes. You are working on the turning chain, so it's not as even as a row; just work the best you can. Fasten off and weave in ends.

## FINISH

Lay Back piece down on flat surface; place both Front Panels on top, line up pieces and edges, whipstitch tog from Point B to Point C according to diagram and whipstitch tog straps.

Approx every 2½"/6cm, sew on a button on the front panel without buttonholes, to correspond with Front Panel with buttonholes.

Designer: **Cecily Keim**

Disco has popped up in one form or another since the '70s. Madonna—my childhood favorite—gave me dance fever with her CD **Confessions on a Dance Floor**. A sequined beanie is perfect for a walk in the park or a roller boogie!

## Size
S/M(L)

## Finished Measurements
Stretches to fit up to 22(24)"/56(61) cm in circumference

## You Will Need
Patons Grace (100% mercerized cotton; 1.75oz/50g = 136yd/125m): 1 skein, color Lilac #60231— approx 136yd/125m of DK-weight yarn, (3)

Berroco Lazer FX (100% nylon; 0.35oz/10g = 70yd/64m): 1 ball, color Jewel Tones #6005—approx 70yd/64m of lace-weight yarn, (0)

Hook: 5mm/H-8 or size needed to obtain gauge

Yarn needle

Stitch marker

## Stitches Used
Chain (ch)

Single crochet (sc)

Half double crochet (hdc)

Double crochet (dc)

Slip stitch (sl st)

## Gauge
*Take time to check your gauge.*

15 dc = 4"/10cm with yarns held together

8 rows = 4"/10cm with yarns held together

## ALL SIZES
With both strands of yarn held together, ch 2.

*Rnd 1*: Work 7 sc into 2nd ch from hook, sl st into the 1st sc to join rnd. Gently pull on the tail to tighten the center. Mark end of rnd with a stitch marker (7 sc).

*Rnd 2*: Ch 3 (counts as 1st dc, here and throughout), work 1 dc into 1st sc, *work 2 dc in next sc; rep from * 5 times more, sl st to 3rd ch in ch 3 to join (14 dc).

*Rnd 3*: Ch 3, work 2 dc into same sp as the sl st, *work dc in next st; work 2 dc in next st; rep from * until 1 st rem, work 1 dc in last st, sl st to 3rd ch in ch 3 to join (21 dc).

**Rnd 4**: Ch 3, work 1 dc into same sp as the sl st, *work 1 dc in next st; work 2 dc in next st; rep from * until 1 st rem, work 1 dc in last st, sl st to 3rd ch in ch 3 to join (31 dc).

**Rnd 5**: Ch 3, work 1 dc into same sp as the sl st, *work 1 dc in each of next 2 sts; work 2 dc in next st; rep from * until 1 st rem, work 1 dc in last st, sl st to 3rd ch in ch 3 to join (41 dc).

**Rnd 6**: Ch 3, work 1 dc into same sp as the sl st, *work 1 dc in each of next 3 sts; work 2 dc in next st; rep from * until 1 st rem, work 1 dc in last st, sl st to 3rd ch in ch 3 to join (51 dc).

**Rnd 7**: Ch 3, work 1 dc into same sp as the sl st, work 1 dc in each of next 4 sts; work 2 dc in next st; rep from * until 1 st rem, work dc in the last st, sl st to 3rd ch in ch 3 to join (61 dc).

**Rnd 8**: Ch 3, work 1 dc into same sp as the sl st, *work 1 dc in each of next 11 sts; work 2 dc in next st; rep from * until 1 st rem, work 1 dc in last st, sl st to 3rd ch in ch 3 to join (66 dc).

## Small/Medium

**Rnds 9–12**: Ch 3, skip 1st st, work 1 dc in each st around, sl st to 3rd ch of ch 3 to join.

**Rnd 13**: Ch 1, *work 1 sc into each of next 5 sts, work sc2tog; rep from * until 3 sts rem, 3 sc, sl st into 1st sc to join rnd (57 sc).

**Rnds 14–15**: Rep Rnd 9.

**Rnd 16**: Ch 1, work 1 hdc into each st of rnd, sl st to 1st hdc to join. Fasten off, weave in ends.

## Large

**Rnd 9**: Ch 3, work 1 dc into same sp as the sl st, work 1 dc in each of next 10 sts, work 2 dc in next st; rep from * until 1 st rem, work 1 dc in the last st, sl st to 3rd ch in ch 3 to join (72 dc).

**Rnd 10**: Ch 3, work 1 dc into same sp as the sl st, *work 1 dc in each of next 11 sts; work 2 dc in next st; rep from * until 1 st rem, work 1 dc in last st, sl st to 3rd ch in ch 3 to join (78 dc).

**Rnds 11–14**: Ch 3, skip 1st st, work 1 dc in each st of rnd, sl st to 3rd ch in ch 3 to join.

**Round 15**: Ch 1, *work 1 sc into each of the next 5 sts, work sc2tog; rep from * until 1 st rem, sl st into the 1st sc to join round (67 sc).

**Rounds 16-17**: Ch 3, skip 1st st, work 1 dc in each st of round, sl st to 3rd ch in the ch 3 to join (67 dc).

**Round 18**: Ch 1, work 1 hdc around, sl st to 1st hdc to join (67 dc). Fasten off and weave in ends.

*Designer:* **Vickie Howell**

Björk's wardrobe collaboration with The Icelandic Love Corporation brought unabashed freeform crochet to the music world. This lily pad neck garland adds comparable sculptural flair to any outfit but remains tame enough to wear offstage.

## Size

One Size Fits All

## Finished Measurements

Length: Approx 67"/170cm

## You Will Need

SWTC Vickie Howell Collection Rock (40% Soysilk, 30% fine wool, 30% hemp; 1.75oz/50g = 109yd/100m): (A), 2 skeins, color Joan #758; (B), 1 skein, color Ani #746—approx 327yd/300m of worsted-weight yarn, ④

Hooks: 5mm/H-8 and 5.5mm/I-9 or size needed to obtain gauge

Yarn needle

## Stitches Used

Chain (ch)

Single crochet (sc)

Double crochet (dc)

Treble crochet (tr)

Slip stitch (sl st)

## Gauge

*Take time to check your gauge.*

16 dc = 4"/10cm using smaller hook

## CIRCLE (MAKE 10)

*Rnd 1*: With A and smaller hook, ch 4 (1st 3 ch count as 1st dc). Work 11 dc in 4th ch from hook, join round with a sl st1st1st (12 dc).

*Rnd 2*: Ch 3 (counts as 1st dc), dc in same st as join. Dc twice in every st to end. Join rnd with a sl st (24 dc).

*Rnd 3*: Rep Rnd 2 (48 dc). Fasten off.

## FLOWER (MAKE 10)

With B and larger hook, ch 2.

*Rnd 1*: Sc 5 times in 2nd ch from hook, join rnd with a sl st (5 sc).

*Rnd 2*: Ch 1, working through BLs only, sc in each st around, join rnd with a sl st.

*Rnd 3*: Ch 4 (counts as 1st tr), work 4 tr in same st as join, [work 5 tr in next st] 4 times, join rnd with a sl st (25 tr).

*Rnd 4*: Ch 1, *sc in next st, tr in next st; rep from * around, join with a sl st. Fasten off, allow last rnd to curl.

## FINISH

Using yarn needle and A, tack a flower onto each circle. Vary placement of flowers from circle to circle. With A and smaller hook, pick up and sc a st at the edge of one of the circles (circle #1) and ch 11. Attach that chain to another circle (circle #2) with a sc. Fasten off. Go back to circle #1, skip two sts from the last chain, pick up and sc a st and ch 11. Attach this chain to circle #2 with a sc. Cont in this manner, connecting one circle after another with two 11-st chains until the garland is complete. Weave in ends.

*Designer:* **Vickie Howell**

## Size

Women's S(M, L, XL, 2X, 3X)

## Finished Measurements

Chest: 36(42, 48, 54, 60, 66)"/
91(107, 122, 137, 152, 168)cm
Length: 39(40, 41, 42, 43, 44)"/
99(102, 104, 107, 109, 112)cm

## You Will Need

SWTC Vickie Howell Collection
Vegas (67% wool, 29% Soysilk,
4% Lurex; 1.75oz/50g = 109yd/
99m): 13(15, 17, 19, 21, 23) skeins,
color Viva Las #422, plus 2 additional skeins for optional belt—
approx 1417(1635, 1853, 2071,
2289, 2507)yd/1287(1485, 1683,
1881, 2079, 2277)m of worsted-
weight yarn, **(4)**

Hooks: 6mm/J-10 and 9mm/N-13
or size needed to obtain gauge

Yarn needle

## Stitches Used

Chain (ch)

Single crochet (sc)

Double crochet (dc)

Slip stitch (sl st)

Arcade Stitch (see next column)

## Gauge

*Take time to check your gauge.*

15 pattern sts = 4"/10cm using
larger hook

4 rows = 4"/10cm using larger hook

A lady may sing the blues,
but the woman who wears this
colorful calf-length coat will
hum along with Erykah Badu
singing about being an orange
moon that shines bright
as she reflects the light
of the sun.

## Pattern Stitch:
## Arcade

*Row 1 (WS):* Ch 1 (counts
as sc), *ch 3, skip 3 sts,
sc in each of the next 3 sts; rep
from *, ending sc in each of last
2 sts. Turn.

*Row 2:* Ch 1, skip 1st sc, *skip 1 sc,
5 dc in ch-3 sp, skip 1 sc, sc in
next sc (center sc of 3); rep from
*, ending sc in ch 1. Turn.

*Row 3:* Ch 2, skip (1 sc, 1 dc), *sc in
each of next 3 dc (center 3 dc of
5), ch 3, skip (1 dc, 1 sc, 1 dc); rep
from * to last group, sc in each
of 3 dc, ch 2, skip 1 dc, sc in ch 1.
Turn.

*Row 4:* Ch 3, skip 1st sc, 2 dc in ch-2
sp, *skip 1 sc, sc in next sc (center
sc of 3), skip 1 sc, 5 dc in ch-3 sp;
rep from *, ending 3 dc under ch
3. Turn.

*Row 5:* Ch 1, skip 1st dc, sc in next
dc, *ch 3, skip (1 dc, 1 sc, 1 dc), sc
in each of next 3 dc (center 3 dc
of 5); rep from *, ending sc in last
dc, sc in 3rd ch of ch 3. Turn.

## BACK

With larger hook, ch 67(79, 91, 103,
115, 127) sts.

*Row 1:* Sc in 2nd ch from hook and
across. Turn.

*Row 2 (RS):* Ch 1, sc across. Turn.

Work Rows 1-5 of patt st once, then rep
Rows 2-5 of patt st until piece measures
17(17 1/2, 18, 18 1/2, 19, 19 1/2)"/
43(44, 46, 47, 48, 50)cm.

Change to smaller hook (for subtle shaping).

Rep Rows 2–5 of patt st twice.

Change back to larger hook.

Cont in established pattern (rep Rows 2–5
of patt st) until piece measures 31(31½, 32,
32½, 33, 33½)"/79(80, 81, 83, 84, 85)cm,
ending with Row 5.

*(continued next page)*

## SHAPE ARMHOLE

*Next RS row (Row 6 of patt st)*: Ch 1, 2 sl st in ch 2, sl st in next 2 sc, skip 1 sc, 5 dc in ch-3 sp, *skip 1 sc, sc in next sc (center of 3), skip 1 sc, 5 dc in ch-3 sp; rep from * to last 5 dc, skip 1 sc, sl st in next sc. Turn.

*Next row*: Ch 1, skip 1 sc in next 3 dc, ch 3, skip (1 dc, 1 sc, 1 dc), sc in each of next 3 dc; rep from * to end. Turn.

Return to established patt (rep Rows 2–5 of patt st) until piece measures 39(40, 41, 42, 43, 44)"/99(102, 104, 107, 109, 112) cm. Fasten off.

## LEFT FRONT

With larger hook, ch 37(43, 49, 55, 61, 67).

*Row 1*: Sc in 2nd ch from hook and across. Turn.

*Row 2*: Ch 1, sc across. Turn.

*Row 3*: Ch 1 (counts as sc), *ch 3, skip 3 sts, sc in each of the next 3 sts; rep from *, ending sc in each of last 2 sts. Turn.

*Row 4*: Ch 1, skip 1st sc, *skip 1 sc, 5 dc in ch-3 sp, skip 1 sc, sc in next sc (center of sc of 3); rep from *, ending sc in ch 1. Turn.

*Row 5*: Ch 2, skip (1 sc, 1 dc), *1 sc in each of next 3 dc (center 3 dc of 5), ch 3, skip (1 dc, 1 sc, 1 dc); rep from * to last group, sc in each of 3 dc, ch 2, skip 1 dc, sc in ch 1. Turn.

*Row 6*: Ch 3, skip 1st sc, 2 dc in ch-2 sp, *skip 1 sc, sc in next sc (center of sc of 3), skip 1 sc, 5 dc in ch-3 sp; rep from *, ending 3 dc under ch 3. Turn.

*Row 7*: Ch 1, skip 1st dc, sc in next dc, *ch 3, skip (1 dc, 1 sc, 1 dc), sc in each of next 3 dc (center 3 dc of 5); rep from *, ending sc in last dc, sc in 3rd ch of ch 3. Turn.

Rep last 4 rows until piece measures 31(31½, 32, 32½, 33, 33½)"/79(80, 81, 83, 84, 85)cm, ending with Row 5.

## SHAPE ARMHOLE/NECKLINE

*Next RS row (Row 6 of patt st)*: Ch 1, 2 sl st in ch 2, sl st in next 2 sc, skip 1 sc, 5 dc, in ch-3 sp, *skip 1, sc in next sc (center sc of 3), skip 1 sc, 5 dc in ch-3 sp; rep from * to last 5 dc, skip 1, sc, sc2tog (next sc and ch). Turn.

*Next row*: Ch 1, skip (1 sc, 1 dc), sc in next 3 dc, *ch 3, skip (1 dc, 1 sc, 1 dc), sc in next 3 sc; rep from * to last group, ch 3, skip (1 dc, 1 sc, 1 dc), sc in next 4 dc. Turn.

*Next row*: Ch 1, skip 1st sc, *skip 1 sc, 5 dc in ch-3 sp, skip 1 sc, 1 sc in next sc; rep from * to last group, 5 dc in ch-3 sp, sc2tog. Turn.

*Next row*: Skip (1 sc, 1 dc), *sc in each of next 3 dc (center 3 dc of 5), ch 3, skip (1 dc, 1 sc, 1 dc); rep from * to last group, sc in each of 3 dc, ch 2, skip 1 dc, sc in ch 1. Turn.

*Next row*: Ch 3, skip 1st sc, 2 dc in ch-2 sp, *skip 1 sc, sc in next sc (center sc of 3), skip 1 sc, 5 dc in ch-3 sp; rep from *, ending dc under ch 3. Turn.

*Next row*: Ch 1, skip 1 dc, sc, skip 1 dc, sc in next 3 dc, *ch 3, skip (1 dc, 1 sc, 1 dc), sc in each of next 3 dc (center 3 dc of 5); rep from *, ending sc in last dc, sc in 3rd ch of ch-3. Turn.

*Next row*: Ch 1, skip 1st sc, *skip 1 sc, 5 dc in ch-3 sp, skip 1 sc, sc in next sc (center sc of 3); rep from * to last group, 5 dc, skip 1 dc, sc in next dc, sc2tog (next dc and ch 1). Turn.

*Next row*: Ch 2, skip (1 sc, 1 dc), *sc in each of next 3 dc (center 3 dc of 5), ch 3, skip (1 dc, 1 sc, 1 dc); rep from * to last group, sc in each of 3 dc, ch 2, skip 1 dc, sc in ch 1. Turn.

*Next row*: Ch 3, skip 1st sc, 2 dc in ch-2 sp, *skip 1 sc, sc in next sc (center sc of 3), skip 1 sc, 5 dc in ch-3 sp; rep from * to last group, ending with dc in ch-3 sp. Turn.

*Next row*: Ch 1, skip 1 dc, sc, skip 1 dc, sc in next 3 dc, *ch 3, skip (1 dc, 1 sc, 1 dc), sc in each of next 3 dc (center 3 dc of 5); rep from *, ending sc in last dc, sc in 3rd ch of ch 3. Turn.

Cont in established patt of Rows 2–5 of patt st until piece measures same as Back. Fasten off.

## RIGHT FRONT
Work as for Left Front, reversing shaping.

## SLEEVES (MAKE 2)
With larger hook, ch 61(67, 67, 73, 73, 79).

*Row 1*: Sc in 2nd ch from hook and across. Turn.

*Row 2*: Ch 1, sc across. Turn.

Rep Row 2 twice more.

Work Rows 2–5 of patt st until piece measures 18(19, 20, 21, 22, 23)"/46(48, 51, 53, 56, 58)cm (ending with Row 7). Fasten off.

## HOOD
With larger hook, ch 61(67, 73, 79, 86, 92).

*Row 1*: Ch 1 (counts as sc), *ch 3, skip 3 ch, sc in each of the next 3 ch; rep from *, ending sc in each of last 2 ch. Turn.

Work Rows 2–5 of patt st until piece measures 18(18½, 19, 19½, 19½, 19½)"/46(47, 48, 50, 50, 50)cm (ending with Row 7). Fasten off.

## TIE BELT (OPTIONAL)
With smaller hook and double strands of yarn, ch 10.

*Row 1*: Sc in 2nd ch from hook and to end. Turn.

*Row 2*: Ch 1, sc across. Turn.

Rep Row 2 until belt measures 64"/163cm or desired length. Fasten off.

## FINISH
Using yarn needle and 1 strand of yarn, seam together shoulders, attach hood and arms, and seam up sides and hood top. With larger hook, pick up loop at the bottom edge of the right front and ch 1. Sc in next st and evenly all the way up the front, around the hood front, and down the left front. Turn. Sc 2 additional rows around. Fasten off. Weave in ends, block if necessary.

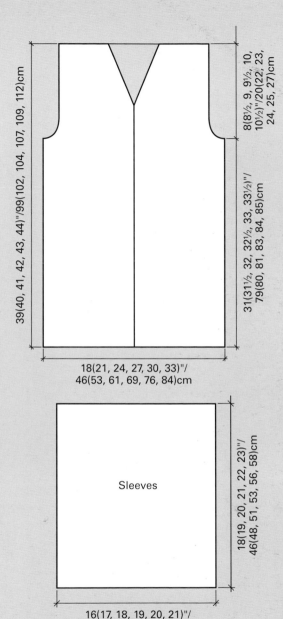

8(8½, 9, 9½, 10, 10½)"/20(22, 23, 24, 25, 27)cm

39(40, 41, 42, 43, 44)"/99(102, 104, 107, 109, 112)cm

31(31½, 32, 32½, 33, 33½)"/79(80, 81, 83, 84, 85)cm

18(21, 24, 27, 30, 33)"/46(53, 61, 69, 76, 84)cm

Sleeves

18(19, 20, 21, 22, 23)"/46(48, 51, 53, 56, 58)cm

16(17, 18, 19, 20, 21)"/41(43, 46, 48, 51, 53)cm

★ ROCKERS ★

# Selena

*Designer:* **Vickie Howell**

This metallic fabric scarf brings out the high school musical star in each of us. Whip it up behind the scenes and have it finished before your next curtain call.

## Size
One Size Fits All

## Finished Measurements
Approx 3¼ x 78"/8 x 198cm

## You Will Need
1 yd/1m of metallic novelty fabric

Hook: 15mm/P or size needed to obtain gauge

Rotary cutter

Quilter's square

Self-healing mat

Yarn needle

## Stitches Used
Chain (ch)

Half double crochet (hdc)

## Gauge
Gauge is not important.

## MAKE FABRIC YARN
Fold fabric in half and then in half again, so you have 4 layers of fabric. Lining up your fabric on the gridlines of the self-healing mat, cut fabric into 1"/3cm strips, using a quilter's square or book as a straight edge to guide you. Don't worry—the strips don't need to be perfect! Tie strips together at ends and wind into ball. You'll notice a lot of fraying at the edges; this will create a great fringed glam look in the finished scarf.

## SCARF
Ch 81.

*Row 1*: Hdc in 3rd ch from hook. Turn.

*Row 2*: Ch 2, hdc to end. Turn.

*Row 3*: Ch 2, hdc to end. Fasten off.

## FINISH
Make sure any ends poking out from your tied strips are firmly knotted. Trim them down to about 2½"/6cm long so you can see the fringe detail of the fabric.

*Designer:* **Sue Rock**

## Size

Women's XS(S, M, L)

## Finished Measurements

Length from wrist to wrist:
52"/132cm (can be adjusted)
Depth at center back: 18(20, 22,
24)"/46(51, 56, 61)cm

## You Will Need

Filatura di Crosa Zara (100% wool;
1.75oz/50g = 136.5yd/124m): (A),
3 skeins, color Black #1404; (B),
3 skeins, color Dark Blue #1389;
(C), 1 skein, color Dark Green
#1888; (D), 1 skein, color Off-
White #1396; (E), 1 skein, color
Red #1449—approx 1229yd/1116m
of DK-weight yarn, ③
Hooks: 5.5mm/I-9 crochet *and*
afghan hook or size needed
to obtain gauge
Yarn needle
Matching thread

## Stitches Used

Chain (ch)
Single crochet (sc)
Double crochet (dc)

## Gauge

*Take time to check your gauge.*
8 mesh sts = 4"/10cm
8 mesh rows = 4"/10cm

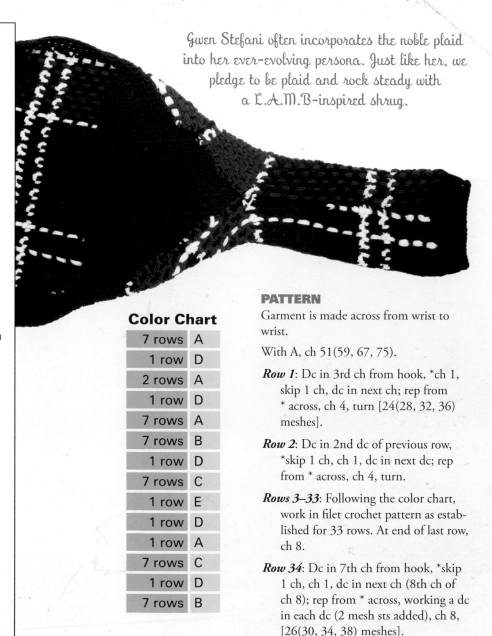

*Gwen Stefani often incorporates the noble plaid into her ever-evolving persona. Just like her, we pledge to be plaid and rock steady with a L.A.M.B-inspired shrug.*

## Color Chart

|  |  |
| --- | --- |
| 7 rows | A |
| 1 row | D |
| 2 rows | A |
| 1 row | D |
| 7 rows | A |
| 7 rows | B |
| 1 row | D |
| 7 rows | C |
| 1 row | E |
| 1 row | D |
| 1 row | A |
| 7 rows | C |
| 1 row | D |
| 7 rows | B |

## PATTERN

Garment is made across from wrist to wrist.

With A, ch 51(59, 67, 75).

***Row 1***: Dc in 3rd ch from hook, *ch 1, skip 1 ch, dc in next ch; rep from * across, ch 4, turn [24(28, 32, 36) meshes].

***Row 2***: Dc in 2nd dc of previous row, *skip 1 ch, ch 1, dc in next dc; rep from * across, ch 4, turn.

***Rows 3–33***: Following the color chart, work in filet crochet pattern as established for 33 rows. At end of last row, ch 8.

***Row 34***: Dc in 7th ch from hook, *skip 1 ch, ch 1, dc in next ch (8th ch of ch 8); rep from * across, working a dc in each dc (2 mesh sts added), ch 8, [26(30, 34, 38) meshes].

*(continued next page)*

*Row 35*: Dc in 7th ch from hook, *skip 1 ch, ch 1, dc in next ch; rep from * across, working a dc in each dc (2 mesh sts added), [28 (32, 36, 40) meshes].

*Rows 36–48*: Work even for 14 rows. On last row, ch 13 (bottom back).

*Row 49*: Dc in 7th ch from hook, *ch 1, skip 1 ch, dc in chain; rep from * across, working last new mesh in 13th ch of ch 13, and completing rest of row as established (4 mesh sts added), ch 4, turn [32 (36, 40, 44) meshes].

*Rows 50–65*: Work in pattern for 25(27, 29, 31) rows. On last row of bottom of shrug crochet 28(32, 36, 40) mesh sts. Ch 4, turn.

*Rows 66–82*: Work in pattern for 16 rows.

*Rows 83–84*: Dec 2 meshes at the beginning of next 2 rows, [24(28, 32, 36) meshes].

*Rows 85 to end*: Work even in pattern for 33 rows. Fasten off; weave in ends.

## TO CHANGE COLORS

Do not ch 4 or turn at end of last row. Make loop on hook with new color, draw it through the loop of last color, and tighten loop of last color. Then with new color, ch 4 and turn.

## TO WEAVE STRIPES

Cut 3 strands of yarn about 12"/30cm longer than the length of mesh (make a loop/slipknot at one end of strands). Starting at the center of the wrist and working from the center of the wrist to the opposite sleeve, weave down through 1 sp and up through next sp to opposite edge of mesh, moving toward the neckline of the garment. On next row, pass same length of yarn over top bar of mesh and start weaving through the next row of spaces, working down to starting edge, being careful to alternate weaving pattern. Follow the color sequence used for creating the mesh (A, D, A, D, A, B, etc.) Remove needle and leave ends until all weaving has been completed.

When weaving has been completed, fold ends over to WS at line of mesh. Then run 2 or 3 rows of machine stitching or backstitch by hand along edge of mesh, catching folded ends of woven strands so they won't pull out.

## FINISH

Fold shrug at arms, sew sleeve seams approx 10"/25 cm from end toward center. Join A, work 4 rnds of sc around body opening. Fasten off. Join A at inner end of sleeve seam (at body opening). Ch 1, sc in same sp, turn. Ch 1, sc 3 times in same st. Ch 1, turn. Continue to work in sc, inc 1 st at each end every other row, until triangle is approx 6"/15cm long. Neatly sew sides of triangle to trim. Rep on other side.

Join A to cuff, work 4 rnds of sc, then 1 rnd in mesh pattern. Fasten off. Rep for 2nd cuff. Weave in ends.

# ABBREVIATIONS

| | | | | |
|---|---|---|---|---|
| **approx** | approximately | | **lp(s)** | loop(s) |
| **beg** | beginning | | **p** | purl |
| **Bet** | between | | **p2tog** | purl two stitches together |
| **BL** | back loop | | **patt** | pattern |
| **BO** | bind off | | **pm** | place marker |
| **BP** | back post | | **prev** | previous |
| **bpdc** | back post double crochet | | **rem** | remain(ing) |
| **ch** | chain | | **rep** | repeat |
| **ch-sp** | chain space | | **rev** | reverse |
| **cl** | cluster | | **rnd(s)** | round(s) |
| **CO** | cast on | | **RS** | right side |
| **cont** | continue(ing) | | **sc** | single crochet |
| **dc** | double crochet | | **sc2tog** | single crochet two stitches together |
| **dc2tog** | double crochet two stitches together | | **sl** | slip |
| **dec** | decrease | | **sl st** | slip stitch |
| **dtr** | double-treble (triple) crochet | | **sp** | space |
| **FL** | front loop | | **ssk** | slip slip knit |
| **FP** | front post | | **st(s)** | stitch(es) |
| **fpdc** | front post double crochet | | **tbl** | through the back loop |
| **hdc** | half double crochet | | **t-ch** | turning chain |
| **hdc2tog** | half double crochet two stitches together | | **tr** | triple (treble) crochet |
| **inc** | increase | | **tss** | Tunisian simple stitch |
| **k** | knit | | **WS** | wrong side |
| **k2tog** | knit two stitches together | | **yo** | yarn over |

## YARN WEIGHT CHART

| YARN WEIGHT SYMBOL & CATEGORY NAMES | **0** lace | **1** super fine | **2** fine | **3** light | **4** medium | **5** bulky | **6** super bulky |
|---|---|---|---|---|---|---|---|
| **TYPE OF YARNS IN CATEGORY** | Fingering, 10-count crochet thread | Sock, Fingering, Baby | Sport, Baby | DK, Light Worsted | Worsted, Afghan, Aran | Chunky, Craft, Rug | Bulky, Roving |

*Source: Craft Yarn Council of America's www.YarnStandards.com*

## CROCHET HOOK EQUIVALENTS

Depending on the material and the manufacturer, several different numbering systems exist for crochet hook sizes. The only constant measurement scale is the metric system, which is often included alongside the size indicator on each hook.

| US Size | Metric |
|---------|--------|
| B-1 | 2.25 mm |
| C-2 | 2.75 mm |
| D-3 | 3.25 mm |
| E-4 | 3.50 mm |
| F-5 | 3.75 mm |
| G-6 | 4.00 mm |
| 7 | 4.50 mm |
| H-8 | 5.00 mm |
| I-9 | 5.50 mm |
| J-10 | 6.00 mm |
| K-10½ | 6.50 mm |
| L-11 | 8.00 mm |
| M/N-13 | 9.00 mm |
| N/P-15 | 10.00 mm |

# About the Designers

**Libby Bailey** is the mother of two (one of whom is Vickie Howell), a grandmother to two, and a high school teacher of American Sign Language and special education (she also ran the school's special ed department for more than a decade). She lives and knits in Lakewood, California.

A lifelong knitter, **Karen Baumer** taught herself to crochet in 2001 when she found a pattern for a crocheted purse that she couldn't live without. In real life, Karen works as a manager of linguistic technology for a California legal consulting firm, and she currently divides her time between San Francisco and Bombay.

Since the age of seventeen, **John Brinegar** has been fascinated by the world of fiber. He initially learned to crochet, but knitting and spinning weren't far behind. After realizing that fiber arts are not only enjoyable but also offer opportunity, John began designing for magazines, including *Vogue Knitting*, *knit.1*, *Knit Simple*, *Crochet Today*, and others. His designs are also featured on Knitty.com, Ravelry.com, and the TV show *Knitty Gritty*. John has taught knitting, crocheting, spinning, and design workshops all over New York City and maintains a studio in Brooklyn, New York. Feel free to visit www.yarnballboogie.com to see the latest information.

**M.K. Carroll's** love of crochet started early and kept her hands busy as a child. She didn't get serious about it, however, until she was confronted with a long bus commute to work; she then started crocheting hats, bags, and bikini tops. Suddenly, she didn't mind getting up early in the morning, or much care about the traffic. Unable to find patterns she liked, her projects were one-of-a-kind confections, gifted to delighted friends. One autumn, after her ears got cold, she knitted hats for weeks, and each one got swapped or purchased right off the hook. It got her to thinking that perhaps it was time for people to crochet her designs for themselves. Her crochet patterns have appeared on crochetme.com, in the books *Stitch 'N Bitch: The Happy Hooker* and *Get Hooked*, and more are available on her blog, mkcarroll.typepad.com.

**Robyn Chachula's** winding path to a career in crochet began, as most do, outside of the industry. She graduated from Penn State University with a degree in architectural engineering and pursued the profession of structural engineer. (Her specialty is historic preservation and renovation.) That day job may seem like a far cry from crochet fashion design, but for her, they're one and the same. They both use her ability to take a big project and break it down into little, easily understood items, then piece them back together to create a complete picture. Her career has also helped her become fluent in crochet symbols, which you see in most of her patterns. Her crochet designs fall in the space between the catwalk and the racks of mid-market retailers.

Robyn designs for the intermediate crocheter who's ready to move on to more challenging projects, but they're still simple enough to ensure success. She's been published in a number of national magazines and books; you can also catch her as a guest on *Knit and Crochet Today* on PBS. Her first two books, *Blueprint Crochet: Modern Designs for the Visual Crocheter* and *Mission Falls Goes Crochet*, were both published in 2008. See all of her architecturally inspired pieces at www.crochetbyfaye.com.

**Stacy Elaine Dacheux** has two adorable nieces named Maddie and Melora, both of whom act as her creative muses. When she's not crafting, she paints, writes, bakes baguettes, or plays with Carver Montacristo, the cat. Her writings appear in *BUST*, *Venus Zine*, the online journal *past simple*, and other small press publications. She currently lives and works in Los Angeles. Visit her online at www.stacyelaine.com.

**Kelley Deal** is the lead guitarist/singer of the band The Breeders, whose much-anticipated album, *Mountain Battles*, was released in spring 2008. When she's not recording, she can usually be found in her hometown of Dayton, Ohio, designing knitted and crocheted handbags. Her first book, *Bags That Rock: Knitting on the Road with Kelley Deal* (Lark Books), hit the shelves in 2008.

**Drew Emborsky's** quirky title as "The Crochet Dude" and his kitschy, tongue-in-cheek designs have made him a household name in the fiber design world. His unique role as a male knitter and crochetier has opened doors for other men stuck in the closet with their yarn, knitting needles, and crochet hooks. Drew studied fine art at Kendall College of Art & Design in Grand Rapids, Michigan. He coauthored *Men Who Knit and the Dogs Who Love Them* (Lark Books, 2007), and his latest book of men's clothing designs in crochet, *The Crochet Dude's Designs for Guys*, was published in 2008 by Lark Books. Drew offers patterns and a peek into his day-to-day life at www.drewemborsky.com. He lives in Houston, Texas, with his two cats, Chandler and Cleocatra.

**Jennifer Fletcher** has been a crafty girl ever since she can remember. Whether she was making dolls with scrap yarn tresses or illustrating her own clothing line for the day when she grew up, she liked working with her hands—and she still does. Today she makes unique jewelry and designs crochet patterns for her website, fablehandmadegoods.com.

**Pam Gilette** can't keep the smile off her face because she's doing exactly what she loves. It's all funky, cool, new, and knotty at www.knottygeneration.com.

**Mary Jane Hall** is an author and a designer of trendy crochet wearables and accessories. You may have seen her trendy designs—57 of which were published her first year of designing in 2005—in various books and magazines. Mary Jane's book, *Positively Crochet!*, is a best seller. Another of her books came out in 2008. She also has two booklets called *Crochet in Style* and *Crochet Young and Trendy*. She's a professional member of CGOA, as well as a member of TNNA. Although she's been a professional singer most of her life, she works full time designing now, and speaks to groups about designing tips and getting published.

**Jennifer Hansen**, aka the Stitch Diva, lives in Fremont, California, where she's a full-time crochet and knit designer, teacher, and writer. Her innovative crochet work has been featured in various books, magazines, and television shows. Her resume includes *Vogue Knitting*, *Interweave Crochet*, *Stitch 'N Bitch: The Happy Hooker*, *Donna Kooler's Encyclopedia of Crochet*, and *Knitty Gritty*. *Yarn Market News* describes her as "one of the names that immediately comes to mind when thinking of the creative forces that have helped transport crochet from the realm of acrylic afghans to the sexy world of figure-flattering fashions." Her professional background is in architecture and information technology. See more of her designs at www.stitchdiva.com.

**Cecily Keim** coauthored *Teach Yourself Visually Crocheting*. She contributes to crochetme.com and *CRAFT Magazine*, and she produces her own video podcast called Such Sweet Hands. You can also find her demonstrating designs on the DIY Network's *Knitty Gritty* and *Uncommon Threads*.

**Edith Beumer Kemp** has been crocheting, knitting, and sewing since kindergarten. She has designed sewing projects for the Elna sewing machine company and taught both basic and decorative sewing classes for more than 10 years. Edie has lived in Austin, Texas, for 35 years and is very grateful for the plethora of non-wool yarns available so she can knit year-round in the Texas heat. She is married to a wonderful man who understands her yarn needs on a deep, deep level, and they have two charming, artistic daughters.

**Whitney Larson** never met a hobby she didn't like. But the pastime that has persisted the longest in her heart is definitely crochet, which she learned at the age of three from her Grannie Bunger. You can read her blog at WhitLarson.com or listen to her podcast at MormonMomCast.com.

Known for the website DisgruntledHousewife.com, **Nikol Lohr** brought her sassmouth to knitting in 2006 with her first book, *Naughty Needles: Sexy, Saucy Patterns for the Bedroom and Beyond*, which she expanded into costumes for an all-knitted burlesque show in 2007. She and artist Ron Miller live and work in the Harveyville Project, a creative residence, workshop space, and retreat housed in beautiful old school buildings in rural Kansas. The Harveyville Project (harveyvilleproject.com) is also home to Yarn School and Felt School, popular weekend crafting retreats. Nikol hearts all things crafty, which you can read about on her craft blog, The Thrifty Knitter (thriftyknitter.com). She's currently working on her second book.

**Sue Rock** is the designer behind Sue Rock Originals EVERYONE Inc., an independent New York design studio of hand-crocheted designs and tailored women's apparel. No stranger to fair trade and green manufacturing, Sue Rock Originals is the first American apparel manufacturer to work with Rwanda Knits, a cooperative working with Rwandan refugees, which recently launched a line of organic llama fiber accessories. As founder of Sue Rock Originals, she provides volunteers with the donated raw materials to create new clothing and accessories for survivors of domestic violence. Since 2005, the company's relationship with Safe Horizon has provided more than 1,000 handcrafted items to women in need.

**Stephanie Ryan's** earliest and most comforting memory is of her grandmother crocheting. With the birth of her own children, she wanted to have something made with her own hands to give her sons, so she returned to her forebear's art. Her gypsy heritage and work in the family engineering business meld in her original crochet designs, which are streamlined but sparkly, flamboyant, and brilliant.

**Jeanette Sherritze** is a professional artist living on the coast of Florida. She began sewing and designing her own garments while very young and transferred that knowledge to knitted and crocheted designs. Her work can be seen at http://knittinginsteadofhousework.blogspot.com.

**Allison Whitlock** has dabbled in most of the needle arts since she was a wee one, but didn't pick up her hooks and needles with serious gusto until she stepped from sunny Sydney, Australia, into the icy winters of the Big Apple. Stitching became her way of whiling away the subway commute and keeping her Aussie bones warm. Of all the needle arts, crochet is one of her faves because it's so fast and free. She rarely sticks to patterns precisely and prefers to use them as a guide and to experiment as she goes. Allison splits her time between Sydney and Los Angeles, where she designs, writes, produces TV, and hosts the DIY Network's needle arts program, *Uncommon Threads*. Online, she shares her craft patterns at www.allisonwhitlock.com and her designs at www.homemademodern.com.

# About the Author

A self-proclaimed crafty grrrl, Vickie Howell has been involved in the creative arts for as long as she can remember.

Before becoming the mother of two boys, Vickie worked in the entertainment industry at companies including International Creative Management (ICM) and Alliance Atlantis Entertainment. Post-motherhood, she's acted as owner, designer, web-mistress, and CEO of three craft-based businesses. Mamarama, founded in 2001, offered cool handmade garb for hip moms and their kids. After relocating to Austin, Texas, in 2003, Vickie cofounded Ruby Goes Retro (RgR) with her sister-in-law. RgR furnished hipsters worldwide with authentic, embellished, and inspired vintage clothing and accessories. In 2005, she founded VickieHowell.com under her company Vickie Howell, Inc., as a home base for her many crafty endeavors. Networking for her businesses led her to nine other crafty entrepreneurs and, together, they cofounded Austin Craft Mafia (ACM), an organization whose sole purpose is to promote and support independent, women-run, craft-based businesses.

In an effort to do her part in the mobilization of the feminist-based knitting movement, Vickie founded successful chapters of the irreverent but socially conscious knitting group Stitch 'n' Bitch in Los Angeles and Austin. Vickie's on a personal quest to assist in breaking the negative social stigma that knitting and crafting have by bringing more recognition to the hip, creative, and edgy sides of these forms of expression. Currently, Vickie can be seen on the DIY Network as the host of the successful knitting series *Knitty Gritty*, and on the Lifetime Television Web series *Crafted*. Her DIY Network one-hour special, *Knitty Gritty Knitsters*, aired in July 2008. She and her ACM partners also debuted *Stylelicious*, another series for DIY that focuses on edgy, handmade fashion.

Vickie, her projects, and her businesses have been featured in such media as *The Today Show*; *USA Today*; E! Network's *Singled Out*; BBC Radio Scotland; *TV Guide*; Knitty.com; the DIY Network's *Jewelry Making* and *Weekend Entertaining*; the magazines *Interweave Knits, Real Simple*, and *BUST*; and the books *Celebrity Scarves 2* and *Tease: Inspired T-shirt Transformations by Superstars of Art, Craft & Design*. She also writes a regular celebrity column for *knit.1* magazine, an eco-craft column for the healthy parenting magazine *KIWI*, and is the knitting editor for CraftGossip.com. In October 2005, her first book, *New Knits on the Block: A Guide to Knitting What Kids Really Want*, hit shelves and was nominated for a Craft Trends Magazine Award of Excellence. In June 2006 came her second book, *Not Another Teen Knitting Book*, followed by her third book, *Knit Aid: A Learn It, Fix It, Finish It Guide for Knitters on the Go*, which debuted in May 2008. Vickie has plans for more books in the future; keep an eye out for them.

Check out Vickie's luxurious, environmentally conscious yarn, the Vickie Howell Collection from Southwest Trading Company, in stores worldwide.

# Acknowledgments

Thanks to everyone at Sterling Publishing for their hard work and continued belief in me, especially to Jo Fagan for delivering me daily doses of humor that only two Irish broads could truly appreciate. I miss you, kid. Thanks also to Marcus Leaver, who went above and beyond his presidential duties to make me feel valued as an artist and author for his company.

To the contributing designers, thank you so much for your beautiful designs and your patience during the multitude of delays that occurred in the development of this book. I appreciate Rebecca Rice for her research and organization, which kept me afloat during this project.

Special thanks for the generosity of the yarn companies Berroco, Moda Dea, Karabella, Crystal Palace, Tahki Stacy Charles, Knit Picks, Lion Brand, Trendsetter, and KFI. I especially thank SWTC, who, during the writing of this book, made a dream come true for me by launching my own line of yarn.

Thanks to my amazing husband, Dave Campbell, to my boys Tanner and Tristan, and to all of my wonderful friends and family for their unconditional love, encouragement, and support—you mean more to me than I have words to describe. I'm a very lucky woman. I love you.

Grateful thanks to the legendary editorial team that worked on this book. At Lark, Kathleen McCafferty, Nathalie Mornu (whose organizational skills blow my mind!), and editorial interns Maggie Alvarez, Courtney Metz, and Katie Henderson all worked diligently to weave in any loose ends. Thanks especially to development editor Valerie Van Arsdale Shrader who saw the potential in this book and nourished it (and me) completely. You all were truly a pleasure to work with!

Thanks to technical editor Amy Polcyn and to proofreader Karen Levy for making sure all the t's got crossed and the i's, dotted.

Special thanks to art director Kristi Pfeffer for making these projects really pop and for so graciously agreeing to listen to my ideas and often implement them (I can't tell you how much that meant to me). Thanks to Stewart O'Shields for his stellar photography. Megan Cox was the right-hand woman during the photo shoot, and the models made looking good look easy…with a little bit of makeup and hair help from Scott Thompson and his assistant Lora Kowalski. Thanks to Dema Badr at Zakya Boutique, Sara Legatski at Honeypot, and Morgan Griggs at Hip Replacements (downtown Asheville, North Carolina, has amazing little shops) and thanks also to Suzie Millions—you all made our styling lives so much easier by generously letting us borrow your wardrobe treasures for the shoot! Orrin Lungren's illustrations make any project a joy to follow. The art production team of Shannon Yokeley, Kelly Stallard, and Jackie Kerr worked together to keep the book on track and gave it celebrity treatment every step of the way. Your tireless work is much appreciated!

# Index

**It's all on www.larkbooks.com**

**Need more pop?**
Check out the Pop Quiz in the Bonus Stuff section.

**Can't find the materials you need to create a project?**
Search our database for craft suppliers & sources for hard-to-find materials.

**Got an idea for a book?**
Read our book proposal guidelines and contact us.

**Want to show off your work?**
Browse current calls for entries.

**Want to know what new and exciting books we're working on?**
Sign up for our free e-newsletter.

**Feeling crafty?**
Find free, downloadable project directions on the site.

**Interested in learning more about the authors, designers & editors who create Lark books?**